A Long & Winding Road

A Journey Through Adoption, Secrets, & Lies

Camille Barnes

Copyright © 2025 by Camille Barnes.

All rights reserved. No part of this publication may be copied, reproduced in any format, by any means, electronic or otherwise, without written permission except in the case of brief quotations in critical articles or reviews.

For more information :

https://www.CamilleBarnesStudio.com

ISBN - Paperback: 979-8-9936105-0-4

ISBN - Hardback : 979-8-9936105-1-1

Table of Contents

Introduction 4
Chapter 1 Where the Road Begins 6
Chapter 2 Detour Through Grief 21
Chapter 3 Even the Wind Was Still 30
Chapter 4 Where Her Road Met Mine 39
Chapter 5 Shadows, Storms, and Sisters 53
Chapter 6 How Did We Get Here 72
Chapter 7 A Sacred Beginning 85
Chapter 8 Pathway through a Dream World 97
Chapter 9 A Journey to the Edge of Sanity 118
Chapter 10 Hope on a Half-Tank of Gas 135
Chapter 11 Detours Toward Belonging 143
Chapter 12 Exit 1991: The Way Home 163
Chapter 13 Stepping into my Miracle 180
Chapter 14 Secrets Left on the Curb 202
Chapter 15 The End of the Road 209
Chapter 16 The Road with No Signs 219
Chapter 17 New Highway Under Construction 229
Chapter 18 Proceed with Caution 241
Chapter 19 I Walk on a Path of Color and Light 261
Chapter 20 The Long Road to the Summit 268
Chapter 21 Highways of Hustle, Byways of Dreaming 274
Chapter 22 Where the Sky Meets the Road 285
Chapter 23 At My Journey's End 293

Dedication

To my family—my husband, my children, and every sibling found along the way, both old and new. And in tender memory of Momma Hazel and Daddy Tommy, whose love still walks beside me, always.

Introduction

We are going to travel the highways and byways, across the bayous, and up toward the summit—the place where wonder opens like a horizon.

For years, I have been gathering scattered pieces of a puzzle, each fragment of memory waiting for its place in the picture of my life.

When the pieces fall together, they form more than an image; they reveal a map. Not a map of land or distance, but one of family, belonging, and the quiet resilience that has carried me through shadows and storms.

This book is that map, a record of where I have been and what I have found along the way. I invite you to walk this pathway with me, a true story. Even when I thought I had reached the end of the road, I discovered new turns, detours, and unexpected construction zones, reminding me that the journey is not finished.

The puzzle of life never fully completes itself; it shifts and rearranges. A signpost rises, a compass point emerges, and you find yourself asking, "does this piece belong here...or is it leading me to someplace I haven't yet imagined?"

Chapter 1

Where the Road Begins

There was once a boy named Tommy, one of five spirited children: Billy, Rai, Dale, Thomas aka Tommy, and Karen, growing up in a house where shadows often fell heavier than sunlight. His father, in his better moments, tried to steady the home with the work of his hands, he was innovative and entrepreneurial. He was a leader in the antique business in the New Orleans area for decades. His family had immigrated to the U.S. from Portugal.

But both of Tommy's parents were caught in the grasp of alcohol, often this slipped into fits of rage. The sounds of fighting became a bitter lullaby. Rent notices gathered like autumn leaves at the door, and the family moved from place to place, never long enough to let roots hold.

Tommy thought of his older brother as the golden child, the one praised when the rare warmth passed through the walls of that fragile house. Together, the two boys made a pact against their world, incredibly mischievous comrades in search of something better.

Rai, Fernand, Billy, Karen, Dale and Tommy

Once, when Tommy was just eight, they stowed away on a train and disappeared into the unknown, carried by wheels that clattered like a heartbeat on iron tracks. It was adventure. Before long, they had reached Baton Rouge, more than 70 miles from home, when the police found them. The story reached the pages of the local Times-Picayune newspaper. According to the article, the boys had stowed away in search of snow, not realizing just how far they would have to travel before finding any.

When Tommy was a young teenager, he had a terrible accident. A student from a nearby college ran a stop sign, and the car plowed into his thin, frail body. The motorcycle went in one direction, and he flew in another. This left Tommy with broken bones and years of recovery in Charity Hospital of New Orleans. Three long years, with few visitors. His world became quiet, filled with white sheets, faint antiseptic smells, and old movies flickering against the walls each Friday night. He would later say it was the movie nights that saved him, that for a few moments, he could escape into stories that always seemed to end better than his own. (With only the exception of one night, when a girl was carried out of the room by men in white coats, screaming at the top of her voice.)

He learned to play the harmonica. Tommy and some of the other young guys would have wheelchair races down the halls of Charity at night when the nuns and nurses weren't around.

He was constantly playing pranks on his fellow buddies and the hospital staff. His love for being mischievous certainly wasn't a bit damaged in the accident.

But now, let us turn down the road and walk another path—the narrow, pine-framed country road that leads to Hazel.

She was born in 1937 at Charity Hospital to Arcy and Johnny Johnson. The family ended up living in the area of Logtown, Mississippi, a place where the woods were thick and the days hard-earned.

Logtown is named after the logs that were once harvested. Located at the mouth of the Pearl River, Logtown was once the site of several sawmills. The Weston Mill halted production in 1930. The town quickly dwindled away.

Hazel came into the world with eyes wide open with wonder. Her beauty was like that of a little cherub, the kind that lingered gently in the memory of those who passed her by. But sorrow found her early. When she was only three months old, her father was taken by the river. He drowned in the wide, unpredictable arms of the Mississippi. Her mother never recovered fully, and the burden of grief and extreme poverty settled heavily on the house.

Arcy and Baby Hazel at the cabin

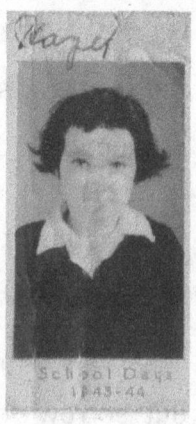

Hazel had two brothers, Raymond and Little Johnny, and the three children grew like wildflowers through cracks in the cement. The family's woes were deep and unrelenting. When they visited their grandma (Rebecca) Long in New Orleans, each of them would get a quarter so they could walk to the movie theatre and see the latest film. Jungle Book was one they all fell in love with—the adventures in the jungle reminded them of Logtown.

Hazel and her brothers would gather old newspapers along the way, sometimes taken quietly from porches not their own. On returning to Logtown, they would press the pages into the cracks of their little cabin's walls and floorboards, trying to keep out the winter wind and the biting insects that came with it.

She remembered when their school began offering free lunches. "At least," she said, smiling, "I knew I would have at least one meal that day."

Hazel learned to survive not just with skill, but with dignity. She fished with quiet patience, went hunting with her brothers, and grew a tiny garden in the patch of sun that touched their yard. She also learned to cook what the land provided: squirrels, birds, frogs, and turtles. Families like hers didn't have the luxury of refusal. They ate what they could get their hands on, sometimes deer, wild hogs, even garfish and alligator. It wasn't always pretty, but it was life, and Hazel bore it with a kind of resilient grace. One of her favorite childhood memories was her pet raccoon, and there was a particular day when she was given an ice cream cone. This was an incredible treat for any girl her age. Out of love for her tiny buddy, she shared her ice cream cone.

The family later relocated to the Irish Channel in New Orleans. The Irish Channel was where many of the Irish in the city lived, they were working-class people, and many were from immigrant families. They lived in shotgun houses. These cottages got their name because you could stand at the front door and shoot a shotgun "clean through" the house to the back door. It's a long and narrow residence, usually about 12' wide. The rooms line up one behind the other with a hallway running down one side.

Living in the city wasn't much easier, but at least Hazel was close to her grandma, whom she loved dearly. They would spend hours together; Grandma was teaching Hazel to sew, to can fruits and vegetables, and to make jelly. The two would go shopping at the farmers' market down by the river to find the freshest of ingredients.

One day, Hazel "got up the guts" to ask Grandma, "Why did you let Momma marry so young?" Arcy was only 13 years old when she married some man named Larson. Grandma Long replied, "Hazel, that girl was so wild, I just was ready for her to go."

But then came a turning point no child should face. Arcy remarried. The man who entered their home did not come with kindness. His presence darkened every room, and his evil cruelty grew bolder with each passing month. When Hazel was thirteen, she was a budding beauty. She had dark hair and stunning eyes. Her skin was as soft as pure silk, and her demeanor was gentle. This horrible stepfather did the unspeakable to her. He stole from her something sacred, something no child should ever have to bear.

She told her mother. But Arcy, broken, hardened, and burdened by life, was in denial. She refused to believe her daughter's story and cries for help. Her mother did nothing to aid, console, or defend her. There was no comfort. No refuge. Just the echo of abandonment that followed Hazel into the quiet corners of her soul.

What followed was not healing, but retreat, a valley of deep despair. Hazel, too tender and too wounded to fight the silence that surrounded her, she began to vanish into herself. Her laughter, once small but sincere, faded. Her appetite disappeared. She walked through the days as though her soul had packed its suitcase and slipped out the door without her. She reached that dark, unspoken place people called a "complete emotional breakdown."

Eventually, her unraveling could no longer be ignored. Hazel was sent away. She was carried by train across Lake Pontchartrain to Mandeville, where the psychiatric hospital sat hidden behind high trees and iron gates. She was still just a girl, a young teenager about the age of 14.

At the hospital, time no longer passed the way it did in the outside world. Days blurred together in the hush of corridors, in the rustle of white gowns, in the quiet cries of other girls whose stories echoed too many painful similarities to her own. There were rules, long walks in circles, and pills passed out. Screams pierced the walls from girls enduring electric shock therapy, a sound that lingered long after it had stopped.

Hazel had a difficult time relating to people, but this time it was different. She had made a friend, the two girls had kindred spirits. Both had endured much hardship, and because of their circumstances, they could relate well to each other. It was like Hazel had a friend who understood her, probably for the first time.

There was also a doctor, who was from uptown New Orleans. Dr. McNeese was his name. He and his wife had no children of their own. Hazel never had the courage to ask why. He was gentle, with a beard that made him look like he belonged in a book of parables. His wife brought homemade cookies on holidays and once slipped Hazel a warm pair of knitted socks. A few times, the good-hearted doctor checked Hazel out for the weekends to come stay at his house. He must have gained her trust because it was extremely difficult for her to trust anyone. Hazel felt safe with the two of them. Their home was like one out of a movie. Not quite like the house in *Gone With The Wind*, but still grand to a destitute girl. People who lived in the poorest sections of New Orleans thought of the people "uptown" like kings and queens in palaces.

One autumn afternoon, as leaves fell outside the sun-drenched window of his office, Dr. McNeese said softly, "If we could, Hazel, we would take you home with us. The laws won't let us. But we care for you."

That was the moment something small and bright cracked through the dark. Not quite hope, but a remembering that such a thing once existed.

After being there for three years, her time at the hospital came to an end. Hazel was given two choices: return to her mother's house, or go to distant relatives up north. She chose the latter. A train ticket was arranged. A suitcase was packed.

Her new home was cleaner, colder not only from the snow but it was void of emotional warmth. She stayed with an aunt and uncle whose affection was as stiff as a starched shirt straight off the ironing board. But she was safe. She was clothed. She was fed.

She learned to work a telephone switchboard, sitting for hours each day with a headset pinched to her face, plugging and unplugging wires, connecting strangers across the city of Indianapolis. The task, though repetitive, brought a quiet peace. The voices were kind. The work predictable.

Hazel was stunning, glamorous when it came to beauty. Often, people would stop her to ask for her autograph because she had an uncanny resemblance to Elizabeth Taylor.

Then one evening, walking home with her coat drawn tight and snow whispering beneath her shoes, a man approached her beneath the glow of a streetlamp. He smiled, a bit too close for comfort, and asked if she was a "working girl."

"Yes," she said innocently, not knowing what he meant.

It wasn't until years later that the memory returned to her with heat and shame. She had been so young. So unaware.

Eventually, the coldness in that house proved too much. The discipline without tenderness. The rules without regard. At twenty, Hazel folded her few belongings and boarded a Greyhound bus headed south. Back to the city of jazz music, streetcars, old iron fences, and magnolias. Back to New Orleans.

Her grandma (Rebecca Long) was still around and could help Hazel out here and there. She stayed with Grandma Long while she searched for work and a small efficiency apartment. She was older now, but still so young in the ways of love.

Then came Mardi Gras.

Hazel, wrapped in a borrowed coat and drawn by the jazz music echoing through the Quarter, wandered into a small bar lit with lanterns and laughter. And that's where she met a guy. He was a real cut-up; his charm was charismatic. He was fun, bold, warm in a way that surprised her. He made her laugh when she didn't think she could. He asked questions and actually waited for the answers. He told her stories that weren't trying to impress—just trying to connect. And somehow, they did.

Three months later, with the scent of jasmine drifting through the windows, they were married by a justice of the peace in the French Quarter courthouse. It's a grand Beaux-Arts-style building from the early 1900s. Not a church wedding, but when you're getting married in the spur of the moment, this place works out pretty well. This guy, by the way, is Tommy, who you learned about earlier.

Hazel, early 20s

In so many ways, they could relate to each other: the dysfunctional families, difficult upbringings, and time spent in hospitals as teenagers. They both loved New Orleans and the deep South: going to the bayou and crabbing, eating seafood at Fitzgerald's on Lake Pontchartrain, late-night strolls to Café Du Monde. They both loved music and dancing. Tommy worked with his father in the antique business. It wasn't a huge amount of money, but it was enough to provide for them.

They found a quaint little house on Murray Street in New Orleans near the Industrial Canal. The levee was visible from their front door. There was a beautiful live oak tree in the backyard and a pretty row of flowers near the front porch. Life seemed to be so much better. Things were on a new path for both of them. They found love. They had hope. And the future looked brighter.

They were two broken people hoping, somehow, to make each other whole.

And the best news came: the doctor said, "Hazel, you are going to have a baby!" She hurried home to tell Tommy the good news. The joy was more than they could have ever imagined. A new baby! They would now have the chance to share their love with another little life. This was something Hazel longed for. But in the back of her mind, she thought that maybe she was damaged goods. She knew she was mentally damaged, but could she also have been physically damaged? Would that horrific day at age 13 destroy her future as severely as it destroyed her past?

Soon the baby belly began to show, and she started making plans for a nursery and looking at sweet little baby clothes each time she walked through a department store.

When you are not yet a parent, you try to imagine how this little child will change your life. What will they be like? What will they look like? A million questions run through your head.

Tommy & Hazel – 1950s

Everything was completely coming together. The two of them were overjoyed.

Chapter 2

Detour Through Grief

Life finally seemed like a "happily ever after". Hazel found a husband that she loved. They were making a beautiful home for themselves and were expecting a baby. She moved through the days as if her heart had finally been given permission to be happy. She folded baby clothes and painted soft colors on the nursery walls. She imagined rocking her baby to lullabies in the quiet hours.

Several months passed by, and then it happened. A "bloody show" which isn't a horror movie, but might as well be. Hazel miscarried. You're walking along, and life is good. Then you're hit, like a punch in the gut that steals the air from your lungs and knocks you to the ground.

As time progresses, you learn, like with anything...pick yourself up and move on. Get over the disappointment and accept what is. Okay, these clichés sound so easy, but there's really nothing easy about them. There are no words to express the disappointment this time... the discouragement, and the depression.

Pick up the broken pieces again. Do your best to act like you are happy and NOT talk about this because talking about it makes it hurt more.

"Hey, let's go buy a new car", Tommy says.

"WOW! Yes, that would be awesome, and go out to dinner." Hazel replies.

It's like putting on a mask and pretending the pain just isn't there. We all do it, but most people do not want to admit it.

She grieved in silence, not wanting to burden Tommy, who had no words for this kind of sorrow. "We'll try again," he said with a hopeful tone. And they did. About seven months later, Hazel is expecting again. But the second time, Hazel didn't allow herself to dream so easily. She kept the nursery door closed. She told herself not to count the days. But hope is stubborn, and when the flutters came, she whispered promises into the darkness: "this time, this time." Yet again, the life within her slipped quietly away. Then came the pain.

Not a sharp pain, but a slow ache that told her something inside her was unraveling. She curled herself on the bathroom floor and listened to her body mourn. No cries left her lips, just quiet breaths, as though speaking it would make it more real.

Tommy found her like that, eyes open, body still.

He sank to the floor beside her and placed his hand on her back. "No," he whispered, over and over again. "No."

But it was.

Tommy, not knowing how to console her enough to make a difference, felt helpless. Instead of "being" there for her, he retreated. He spent more and more nights away from home, out with the guys. This was becoming a routine now, even on good and "happy" days. Neglect is abuse, even when you don't recognize it as such.

The following year, a "rabbit test" confirmed: Pregnant. Yes. Again. The rabbit test was a human pregnancy test developed in 1931, in which urine from a woman would be injected into a female rabbit. The rabbit would be dissected, and if its ovaries were enlarged, then the woman was probably pregnant. This had a 98% certainty. A common euphemism people would say is "The rabbit died" meaning the test was positive. The test was used into the 1970s.

Okay, Hazel told herself, this time will be different. I will slow down my pace, be careful with everything I do, and eat more fresh fruit and vegetables. Don't let your excitement be too zealous. Brace yourself for what could happen and take it one day at a time.

Alright, the first month went great. Yay! Second month...all is well. She sat beneath the oak tree and whispered into the branches, "God, please... just this once."

During the third month, Tommy gets an idea, one Saturday morning, that would be so adventurous for them. "Let's get outta here," he said. "Let's go down to Lafitte and buy a boat. We will go to the bayou like we used to. We're gonna fish on the weekends and troll through the bayou. Don't worry,

Hazel, I won't go very fast."

She agreed to go. They found a boat, it was small, but fast.

The fourth month, everything is great. The days passed slowly and carefully. Hazel counted them like beads on a rosary. She kept her heart guarded, but the hope pressed forward like green shoots breaking through hard soil.

She's beginning to feel the "flutters". Then, she began to ponder the questions again... not a million, let's stick to a thousand or so. Fifth month...good. "I feel little baby kicks, for sure this time, Tommy." Laughter was in the house again. She danced around the kitchen again. Tommy pressed his ear to her belly, and she watched his eyes shine. The nursery was reopened. The little blue sweater lay out. Thanksgiving arrived in a whirl of laughter, sticky fingers, and the relentless chatter of nieces and nephews. Hazel held a particular fondness for her little nieces—Marion, Debra, and Donna. In their presence, joy seemed effortless, bubbling up around her. She smiled through the chaos, cradling not just their small hands, but the delicate hope that this fleeting happiness might endure a little longer.

And then Hazel's little nephew, Terry, about four years old, came barreling in behind the girls, scaring them half to death with his roaring laughter. His cowboy hat pulled down low, and his boots clomping like thunder on the floorboards. He was a cowboy through and through. That little freckled face of his beamed beneath the brim, proud as could be. There was something about the way he charged into a room, half wild, half wonderful, that made you want to laugh and hold onto the moment forever.

Six months: bigger baby belly, more excitement creeps in.

Tommy's lifestyle was becoming more about drinking and gambling than becoming a family man, though. There's a baby on the way, and it will be here soon. Hazel doesn't want to confront him about his habits because when he is around, he is being kind, as she doesn't want to "rock the boat," especially since the new boat is making him this happy.

The doctor says everything looks great, your baby is due to arrive in January, just after the holidays.

They rode out to the marshes at sunset, the cypress trees casting long shadows across the water. Hazel laughed, truly laughed, as wind tangled her hair. Tommy reached for her hand and for a moment, they remembered what it felt like to be whole.

But the next week, the nausea came back.

She thought it was the boat, the motion. She told herself it was just the movement of the water, but her heart knew. The child within her womb had stopped kicking.

She made an appointment at the clinic; the doctor confirmed her fears. The doctor had kind eyes and gently said, "I'm so sorry". But the words fell flat. Hazel had heard them before. Three times now. And each time, they scraped something deeper.

Tommy hadn't known what to say. So, he didn't. He just left that night, leaving Hazel all alone once again.

There was no script for this kind of sorrow. No polite words. Just an ache that settled into the corners of the house, into the folds of their marriage and into the very way she breathed.

It was a cold, dark, and rainy night. As Hazel was home alone, She paced the floors again, worrying about him and looking out the windows to see if that was his truck she heard outside. Where was he? (All of the usual questions.) It's 1960, there are no cell phones and no beepers invented yet. If the person you're worried about doesn't find a pay phone or borrow someone's landline to call you, there's nothing you can do but hope and pray they are okay.

Later in the night, he called to say he was out getting some drinks and shooting some pool. Just go to sleep. I have no idea when I will be home.

The rain slipped down the windowpanes like tears, blurring the view of the levee beyond the porch. Wind rustled through the live oak in the backyard, and every now and then the branches scraped against the glass like restless fingers searching for solace. The old house creaked with each gust, as if it too, was weary from holding grief.

Hazel sat curled beneath an old quilt, her teacup untouched. The warmth had long since fled. Her eyes burned from crying, though no tears came now. Grief had hollowed her, emptied her of everything except the aching silence. Hope deferred makes the heart sick. Tommy found her when he came back home. He didn't say a word. They didn't talk about it afterward. They couldn't. Some grief is too vast for words.

The boat sat under its tarp. The "new boat smell" reminded them of everything they'd lost.

The nursery door down the hall closed. She remembered pressing Tommy's hand to her belly just days before the loss. The way his face lit up when he felt the movement. "That's our baby," he whispered. And for a moment, she let herself believe in miracles.

By Thanksgiving, the house was full of noise again. Nieces and nephews tumbled through the door with sticky fingers and loud laughter. Hazel smiled through the meal. She even danced in the kitchen with little Donna standing on her feet.

She dared to believe.

Another pain. Another silence. Another ending.

When Tommy went to the bar, he thought this was gonna be like any other night drinking and gambling, but this night changed their lives.

Chapter 3

Even the Wind Was Still

The morning after the rain arrived quietly, without apology. Hazel rose before the sun had fully lifted its head; the sky outside was still bruised with streaks of gray. The rain had passed, but its presence lingered—dripping down the windows, and leaving behind that familiar musty scent that only the humid South can hold like a secret.

She lit a candle in the kitchen, the match sparking like a tiny thunderclap in the stillness. The soft flame wavered against the walls, casting long shadows across the pale cabinets. It flickered beside her as she stirred a splash of cream into her coffee—clockwise, then again, slower this time, until the swirl vanished into something warm and whole. A faint lemon scent drifted up from the bowl of fruit on the table, its brightness a quiet defiance against the damp morning air.

The house was still, as if it too had drawn in a breath and was holding it gently. But this silence wasn't the kind that crushed. It was tender. Spacious. It offered a kind of pause, like the moment between the last note of a lullaby and the hush that follows.

Tommy had gone out early. He hadn't said where, and she hadn't asked. Lately, the space between their words had grown longer, more uncertain, like a rope stretching taut between two boats drifting in opposite directions. She wasn't angry. Just tired.

A deep, bone-level tired. The kind that didn't come from lack of sleep, but from carrying heavy invisible things, grief, disappointment and questions that never got answered. She often wondered if he felt it too, or if he simply drank it away. There were days she didn't recognize the quiet in her own chest, days she wished someone would ask, "Are you alright?" and mean it. But even if they had, she wasn't sure she'd know what to say.

Hazel sat at the table, still in her bathrobe, her fingers curled around the warm mug. She watched the steam rise and twist as if it were dancing its way into the air. In that moment, she whispered a prayer, as if her breath could carry her thoughts into the sky and be heard by someone who understood. Lately, it felt like she whispered only to herself.

You know that feeling, don't you? Like you're floating out in the great expansive universe with no one on the other end of the line. No echo, no nod, no one really seeing you for who you are. You can be surrounded by people and still feel like you're invisible. There's this deep-down ache, not for attention, but for understanding. To be known, without needing to explain every corner of yourself. But that moment rarely comes. And so you just keep going, quietly hoping someone, someday, might actually get it.

Somewhere in the half-sleep of the night, a verse had floated into her mind, it was something about beauty for ashes. It came soft and unbidden, like a feather brushing across the soul. She couldn't recall where she'd heard it, maybe one of the sermons back at the Catholic church from years ago. She didn't carry much scripture in her head, but every now and then a verse would rise up inside her, uninvited, like a melody she hadn't heard in years, playing faintly in the back of her mind. She didn't understand it entirely, but she understood enough: that something broken could one day be made beautiful. That sorrow, somehow, wasn't the end of the story.

And yet, part of her wasn't sure. Part of her wanted to believe that ashes could bloom into something new. But the rest of her had been let down too many times. The empty crib. The stitched-together smiles. The echoing quiet when Tommy came home too late to explain.

Still, she whispered the words again in her mind. Not as a declaration, but as a plea. "Beauty for ashes." Maybe she wasn't there yet. Perhaps she didn't even know how. But she was still here. And maybe, just maybe, that counted for something.

Isn't it strange how a thought can rise up out of nowhere, uninvited, unplanned, especially when your mind is already tangled with a hundred other things? It's like the soul whispers when the mind is too busy to argue. Where did that come from? Hazel didn't know. But there it was.

Another verse drifted into her heart, gentle as the morning sunlight moving through lace curtains: "He restoreth my soul." She hadn't thought of those words in years. Maybe they'd once hung on a plaque in someone's hallway, or echoed from someone in some far-off chapel. Still, they came now with a weight that felt almost sacred. They rested on her spirit , soft, light, and real.

He restoreth my soul.

Could that be true? That a soul worn thin by grief and time, could be restored, not patched or hidden, but truly, deeply restored?

She breathed in, closed her eyes, and let the possibility bloom. It wasn't just a memory of scripture. It was something closer to a touch. A mercy. And oh, how beautiful a mercy it would be.

Later, she opened the nursery door. Just a slow step into a room that remembered things she was still trying to forget.

The little blue sweater still hung on the hook. She folded it gently and placed it in a drawer. Not to erase the memory, but to give it rest.

The blanket on the crib was smoothed. The window was opened. Light poured in. Hazel stood in it, arms crossed, letting the warmth wash over her face. For a moment, she was not grieving. She was simply standing.

By afternoon, she put on a cotton dress and tied her hair back. She found the keys to the car and drove toward the lake, windows down, letting the wind undo the strands of her composure.

The road curved and hummed beneath her. Spanish moss swayed overhead. The world was still here, she realized. It hadn't ended, though parts of her had.

She pulled off the main road onto the familiar gravel patch just past mile marker seventeen, where a little wooden stand sat shaded beneath a sprawling pecan tree. It was one of those places that hadn't changed in years—hand-painted signs, baskets of fresh fruit lined up like a rainbow of effort, and the sweet, earthy smell of sun-warmed produce hanging in the air. Ms. Norma was there, as always, wiping her hands on her apron and humming an old hymn under her breath.

She had a modest farm near Ponchatoula and made the long drive once a week to sell her strawberries, tomatoes, and whatever else the soil had been generous with.

Hazel stepped out of the car and walked over slowly, letting the warm breeze play with the hem of her dress. She picked out a small basket of strawberries, deep red, still dusted with the memory of morning dew, and handed over a few crumpled bills. Ms. Norma looked at her for a long moment, her eyes soft and wise in the way women get when they've weathered their own storms.

"You know," she said, pausing as she tucked the bills into her tin box, "your eyes look clearer today."

Hazel blinked, caught off guard by the observation. No one had said anything like that in a long time. Not since the loss. Not since the sadness had settled into her features like a permanent shadow.

And now here was Ms. Norma, standing beneath a creaky hand-painted sign that read "Sweetest Strawberries in the Parish," was seeing past the surface into Hazel's soul.

Hazel didn't say much in return, she just nodded, her lips

curling into a faint smile. But those words stayed with her the whole drive, like a hand gently pressed against her back, urging her forward.

She drove to Fort Pike.

The ruins stood quiet as ever, watchful, familiar. She walked among the stones, not for answers, but for stillness. She sat beneath a tree where light sifted through branches like grace through sorrow.

In her notebook, she wrote:

"I am not okay. But I am upright. I am not joyful. But I am not destroyed." Sometimes, a little escape does the heart good.

When she came home, Tommy was in the yard working on the boat. The tarp had been pulled back. He was scrubbing the sides, not with urgency, but with care. He looked up when she pulled in. There was something in his eyes that hadn't been there for weeks.

"Thought I'd get it ready," he said. "Maybe a little ride this weekend."

Hazel smiled; the kind that comes from deep in the chest.

"I'd like that." Turning around she hollered out "Ya jeet-jet?" Tommy replied, "No, jew?" * Hazel: "No, I'm fixinto make some grub."

That night, they ate dinner at the table with music playing softly on the radio. Hazel lit another candle. The flame flickered the same way, but the air around it was different. Not whole. Not healed. But less heavy.

Before bed, Tommy stood in the doorway of the nursery. He didn't step inside. He just looked.

"She would've had your eyes," he said. Hazel joined in, "or your smile." They stood side by side in the doorway. Not reaching for what was lost. But finally, letting it rest.

Local-ism vocabulary meanings:

"Did you eat yet?" "No, Did you?"

Chapter 4

Where Her Road Met Mine

Though they had found a fragile rhythm in their quiet life, Tommy's restlessness began to stir again. He missed the hum of late-night bars, the laughter, the music, the pool tables lit in amber haze. He got the adrenaline rush he needed to move forward. The places he went had an excitement he longed for. There was a pulse there, a charge in the air that made him feel alive. Maybe it reminded him of the wild, reckless freedom he once shared with his brother Billy, back when trouble was a kind of game and the future didn't yet feel like a weight.

One evening, Tommy walked into his favorite bar expecting just another night. A drink, a wager, a little noise to drown out the chatter in his head..." the couldof, wouldofs, shouldofs". But what started as routine would alter the course of their lives.

He came home in the late hours of the night, long after the lights in the house had gone dark. He moved quietly into the bedroom, a trace of excitement in his steps as if the night had handed him something he couldn't wait to share. He leaned down beside Hazel, brushed the hair from her face, and whispered, "You just might be a mommy soon." His words floated through the air like the silence of a feather.

That very evening, he had played a game of pool with a guy named Paul Schroeder. Strangers at first, but as the game went on, conversation drifted from casual bets to confessions. Paul, somewhere between shots, began talking about his girl, Terri. Paul said she was young, overwhelmed, already raising two boys, and now pregnant again. She didn't think she could do it all, not alone.

And so, another path opened on this winding road.

Let's take a detour into her story now.

Jane Teresa Brenner Holter—she liked to be called Terri, and would one day also be known as Miriam. She was another soul written into this map of intersecting lives. Like interstates that twist around each other, her story would draw near to Hazel's in ways neither could yet see.

Some threads of fate are sewn softly, like whispers in the dark. Others roar like engines headed for places that don't yet have names.

Terri had lost her mother far too soon.

With several brothers and a father who worked long hours, the weight of the household had quietly fallen onto her young shoulders. The only girl in a house full of guys, she became the one who scrubbed the pots, folded the clothes, and quieted the noise. No one said it outright, but it was understood—this was her role now.

The chores piled up like bricks, each one heavier than the last. Without her mother, the house lost its softness. Terri lost her footing.

And so, she ran away.

She left with a Navy boy named Robert Holter. He had a steadiness to him, the kind that made you feel like the world might actually stop spinning if he held your hand long enough. He had a quiet voice, strong arms, and the kind of look that made a girl believe in second chances. He didn't ask for much. Just her heart. And she gave it, because it felt like rescue.

They traveled to many places, chasing stability on shifting ground. In 1958, their first son, Forrest, was born in Corpus Christi, Texas. Terri still remembered the way the Gulf breeze came through the hospital window and how Robert stood beside her with wide, tender eyes that softened when Forrest let out his first cry. A year later, in 1959, Keith arrived in Minneapolis, Minnesota. That hospital stay was colder, snow flurries on the windowsill. She held her babies close, wrapping them in the only warmth she had to give: herself.

For a while, it seemed like a kind of peace had come. The boys brought structure, purpose, and a new kind of joy. Robert was still quiet, but his presence filled the room. There were early morning feedings and afternoons folding laundry while the radio played something soft in the background. She'd hum lullabies she barely remembered learning. It wasn't perfect—but it felt like life had finally let her exhale.

But then Robert vanished. Gone without warning. Gone without reason. Gone without a trace. His absence left a silence more deafening than any storm. The boys were told he was declared missing and eventually declared dead. What truly happened, no one could say. The questions hung in the air.

By 1960, Terri found herself in New Orleans—young, alone, pregnant again. She confided in her new boyfriend that the weight of the world had settled on her. She said, "I have two children already, a third on the way, and no clear path forward. Maybe I can't do this again. I think I need to give my baby away."

New Orleans had a way of cradling the lost and luring the weary with its jazz-soaked corners and back-alley mystique. The city didn't ask questions. It just played its trumpet and said, laissez les bons temps rouler. (Let the good times roll)

To a girl like Terri, fresh from loss and heavy with the weight of two toddlers, the Crescent City offered more than escape. It offered possibilities.

Mardi Gras had sounded like pure magic to her ears when she first heard about it—an explosion of color, brass bands, beads flung like confetti dreams. The parades, the costumes, the wild joy—it all called to the barefoot part of her spirit. The part that wanted to dance in the street with strangers, to belong somewhere, to forget the ache in her chest for just one night.

Terri had a free bird spirit, or at least that of a butterfly. She moved into an apartment in the French Quarter, close enough to hear the train tracks at night and smell café au lait from the Café du Monde. Her neighbors were a melting pot of misfits: a bearded poet who played bongo drums on his porch, a woman named Starshine who made pottery under a string of Christmas lights year-round, and a Vietnam vet who carved little animals from driftwood and sold them at the French Market. None of them had much, but they shared what they had: gumbo, guitars, and stories that stretched the truth like taffy. One of her neighbors was Al Hirt. He was working a lot in the Nola music scenes, and getting well known throughout the United States.

Terri soon found herself caught up in the warm haze of the city's beatnik and budding hippie culture. She began painting in Jackson Square on the weekends; it was a kind of sacred ground—guitarists strumming folk tunes, barefoot dancers spinning in slow circles, incense smoke curling into the open air. She met girls who wore their hearts on their sleeves and boys who thought the stars held answers. They called each other "cat" and "chick," tossed around words like "far out" and "groovy," and believed that love might actually be the revolution they were all looking for.

It was messy, imperfect, and sometimes they were just plain broke, but Terri had never felt more seen.

People shared what little they had and listened without judgment. She'd bring Forrest and Keith in tow, two little blond-headed boys tugging at her hem while she sat cross-legged in the park, talking about soul journeys and poetry with girls who painted peace signs on their jeans. Nobody cared if she was a single mom or if her eyes still carried too much shadow. In that odd little circle of free spirits and forgotten people, Terri found a strange, welcome kind of comfort. Maybe not a future, but a place to land.

Still, life pressed in. The rent needed to be paid. The fridge didn't stock itself. And Terri, for all her flower-child softness, was still just a girl trying to carry too much on her thin shoulders.

She found a new boyfriend, Paul, to whom she bare her soul. And on one humid evening, the weight of the world had finally settled. Her baby belly was getting bigger, and a cold Christmas loomed just around the corner. I can hardly pay my bills, let alone get Christmas gifts for my boys. This baby is due in March, and I just don't know how to manage with another mouth to feed, and no clear path forward," she said, eyes clouded but calm. "Maybe I can't do this again. I think I need to give my baby away."

Paul didn't answer right away. He just sat there, staring at the bugs circling the porch light like they were chasing answers too. He wasn't ready to take on a commitment like marriage or prepared to be a daddy. Compassion weighed heavily on him as he saw the struggles she faced.

A few weeks after the holidays, Paul found himself at a downtown bar and met a guy who was unusually good at pool, Tommy. Each of these guys had a pretty good competitive spirit when it came to this game.

They began playing every night. One evening, Paul leaned

over the green felt and told his new friend, the story of a girl named Terri —not with drama, but with the quiet urgency of someone carrying someone else's burden. A young woman, already raising two little boys, is now pregnant again. She's a girl who had too much heart and not enough help. Worn thin. Worn quiet. Life had her cornered, and she was trying to find a way forward that wouldn't drown her. "She's thinking about giving the baby up," Paul said. "Not because she doesn't care. Just the opposite. She cares so much, and she knows she's out of options."

Paul told Tommy all this that very night. And something stirred in Tommy. He told Paul about all of the miscarriages and how devastated his wife was. I see her living in agony every day, and I just want to help her.

And that story, that one conversation, would turn the gears of fate.

That night, something stirred in Tommy.

This would be the beginning of my story.

A winding road of chance and grace, filled with twists, turns, and potholes, long before I ever took my first breath. A road filled full of detours and broken signs, long before I ever arrived.

Tommy sold his boat—the one they had bought in better days—just to cover the legal fees of this private adoption. And in March of 1961...

I was born.

Hi, I'm Camille. Hazel became my mother just weeks after she lost her last pregnancy. I wasn't born of her body, but I was born straight into the open hands of her prayers. She told me the story a hundred times as I grew. And every time, her eyes glistened with the same quiet joy.

"Camille," she'd say, "I always wanted a baby. I cried, and I prayed, and every time I got pregnant, I lost the baby. It broke my heart in ways I can't explain. Still, I kept praying. I begged God for a child... and then you came into my life."

Terri had two little boys already, and Hazel, my new mother, offered to babysit them while Terri went into the Sara Mayo hospital to give birth. Three days later, they brought me home.

Most people thought I was Hazel's own. In many ways, I was. Her body still bore the shape of the child she had expected in January.

What I do remember about those early years is how golden they felt.

Hazel and Tommy finally had the child they had prayed for, longed for, and nearly given up hoping for. I felt loved, chosen, treasured.

Momma Hazel named me after the girl she knew while living in the mental hospital. Camille was a true friend, but a very sad girl. She ended up committing suicide. Hazel was broken when she received the news that her friend had died so tragically, and made a promise to herself that "if I ever have a baby girl, I will name her Camille, and give her a better life than my friend had." Our little house, nestled by the levee, was filled with warmth and laughter. I remember sunshine spilling through the windows and glistening on the old wood floors, and the sound of music echoing down the hallway. I remember flying a kite with my daddy one bright spring day, the two of us chasing the wind up on the levee, the sky wide and blue above us.

I remember dancing in the living room with Momma when American Bandstand came on the TV. She'd take my hands and twirl me around, our laughter rising with the music. We'd watch Romper Room, Johnny's Follies, Mr. Magoo, and one of my favorites: Red Skelton—each show its own little moment of magic in the rhythm of our days.

I have this faint memory of sneaking Daddy's cartons of cigarettes and stashing them in the oven. One day, Momma decided to bake a pie, preheated the oven, and—surprise!—the smell of whole stacks of cigarettes cooking filled the house. Smoke everywhere. Let's just say I had developed a healthy hatred for Daddy's smoking habit.

One day, he dared me, "Well, go on then—take a puff." I did. I hacked, my eyes watered, my throat burned, and my Momma was furious with him. But later in life, when other kids tried to act cool by lighting up, I thought to myself, you can be cool and be a fool if you want to be, but I'm not about to do that.

Over time, I came to understand how adoption usually works. I learned how agencies carefully vet each hopeful parent, sifting through applications, conducting interviews, checking boxes. It's a system built to protect children, to ensure they're placed in safe, stable homes.

Truth be told, I don't think my parents would've passed that kind of scrutiny. On paper, they might have fallen short.

It worked out for them to get me the way that they did.

The past is ever whispering to us. Mine is filled with the stories Momma told me.

Momma used to tell me stories about Keith and Forrest, the two boys who were my big brothers. She had taken some photos of them when they stayed with her and tucked them away into an old envelope to be given to me one day. Keith was the bubbly one, smiling and playing. Forrest was quiet; he kept to himself. At times, it seemed like that little boy had the weight of the world on his shoulders. And his nickname is Woody. She would tell me how precious they were, and I began to love them. And then she'd tell me about Terri herself.

"She's a real hippie girl," she'd say with a little laugh mixed with complete sarcasm, "quiet and soft-spoken, with dark hair and a way of swirling her cigarette around in one of those long holders like she was something cute and special."

And in a way, she was. Because her road met Hazel's.

Chapter 5

Shadows, Storms, and Sisters

When I tell you about the people in my life, and it seems to reveal them in a negative light, it's not to criticize them. I would like you to understand the level of deep darkness and dysfunctional attributes that surrounded me as a child. I lived with a sense of hopelessness and despair off and on for many years. Like with most people, my story begins with "my parents" stories because they are the ones with the most powerful influence in our formative years.

I always remembered my early years as happy ones. The house felt warm, laughter came easily, and I don't recall any fighting. But there were shadows, quiet, unexplained things that crept in while the world slept. My daddy would stay away many nights and not come home; I was too young to understand why. I only knew I wanted him home.

Our next-door neighbors were an elderly couple. Mr. Matthew and I would play soldiers for what felt like hours—though in reality, time probably crawled. He had the old cast-iron kind, each about an inch tall, and we would line the entire living room floor, carefully arranging them for battle. Meanwhile, his wife, Ms. Virginia, baked homemade cookies for us, filling the house with warmth and sugar-sweet smells. Their dog, Mr. Bandit, was exiled to a bedroom down the hall, because he had a habit of knocking over my tiny army. They were the first friends I ever had, and I loved every minute of being at their house.

The Beginning of My Artistic Journey

Sanchez Antique Gallery on Charters Street, French Quarter

My love of masterful craftsmanship was born in the half-light of memory, inside my father and grandfather's antique gallery. To me, that place was a kingdom—each relic humming with meaning. My dad moved through it like Jean

Lafitte himself, a pirate with a nose for beauty, chasing treasures as though they were gold.

I was small, but I wandered those aisles as if they were cathedral halls. My eyes traced the gleam of opera glasses that glittered like captured stars, the soft shine of silver hairbrushes etched with patience so fine it felt like prayer. These were not simply things. They were stories forged into matter, voices from another century whispering through brass, silver, and glass.

What captivated me most wasn't just their elegance, but the devotion folded into them, the unseen hands that shaped them, the reverence pressed into every detail. It was there, in those shadows, that my own longing was born: to create work that could hush a room, still the noise, and stir the hidden places of the heart.

Momma Hazel loved to remind me that when I was four, someone placed a few coins in my hand. I looked up at her, wide-eyed and certain, and declared, "Mommy, now I need to go buy some art supplies."

What began as wonder in my father's gallery soon rooted itself as desire. By the time I was five, I was already saving spare change to buy art supplies. No teacher, no lessons—just instinct and an unrelenting hunger to create. I taught myself with whatever I had.

Even as a child, I earned my nickels, dimes, and quarters. Once a month, Sanchez Antiques on Magazine Street transformed into a theater of wonder. Notices were placed in the classified section of the Times-Picayune—back when "going viral" meant your ad might get circled in red ink. Dealers from every corner gathered to bid on tester beds, armoires, sideboards, silver, sculptures, and paintings, pieces grand enough to rival any museum. My father sat high in the booth like a king on his throne, calling out the rhythm of bids, his hand flying across the page as paddle numbers claimed their prizes.

My "big girl job" was simple but solemn: to carry those finished sheets to my mother in the office, my small hands passing along the record of treasures lost and found. It was my first taste of responsibility, my first coins earned in the house of beauty.

My first oil painting was of our dog, Happy. Awkward and muddy though it was, to me it was everything. I couldn't wait to show it to my family, bursting with pride as they sat gathered around the television, eyes fixed on Bonanza or Mayberry, or whatever was on that night. No one looked up. Still, the spark didn't die. If anything, it burned brighter, quietly, stubbornly, the way a dream begins.

In that solitude, I began to grow—not just in skill, but in spirit. My art became a sanctuary, a place where I didn't need permission to create beauty. It became my quiet devotion, a place to whisper my prayers. Late at night, after homework, housework, and tucking the younger ones into bed, I would retreat to my desk. In the glow of a single lamp, I came alive—painting, studying, chasing light and shadow with the urgency of someone who knew it mattered.

Those early nights—just me, the paint, and the silence, were where I learned not only to see, but to believe.

In 1964, Hazel became pregnant again. And this time... there was no miscarriage. In January 1965, I was no longer an only child. I had a baby sister. "My baby" Becky.

At first, I thought this new chapter would be wonderful. (It was, in many ways.) But after four years of having my parents' full attention, their whole hearts wrapped around me, the adjustment wasn't easy. Now there was a baby that looked like them. Blood of their blood. The excitement in the house was undeniable. A new life. A new miracle.

To make room for the growing family, Tommy and Hazel put a deposit down on a brand-new house. It was on the West Bank of the river, near farm yards and horses. It was still being built, a fresh start, filled with dreams, plans, and hopeful rooms not yet painted.

But let's make a little U-turn here.

Before the move, on the night of September 9, 1965, Hurricane Betsy struck New Orleans with a fury the city had never seen. It was a Category 4 storm, roaring in with winds up to 160 miles per hour.

That night, I lay in my parents' bed with Momma and my baby. The windows rattled, and our power had gone out. Tree limbs banged against the house. You could hear things smashing in the dark outside. A single candle flickered. The room felt small and terrifying.

Daddy wasn't home, and all phone lines were down. The wind howled outside like a living thing, or a monster. I waited; eyes fixed on the door.

Wasn't he coming home for us? Why wasn't he here?

He had been out so many nights before, but this night was different. This night, we needed him. The world felt big and dangerous that night. I was small, clinging to my mother. I can't even imagine the fear she was facing.

Suddenly, there was a pounding on the front door. Men's voices, urgent and loud— "OPEN THE DOOR!!! Open the door now, or we will break it down!"

The next thing I remember was being lifted into strong arms. A soldier, part of the Louisiana National Guard, was carrying me. The water reached up to his waist as he waded through our street. He placed us gently in the back of a large military truck, the kind covered with camouflage canvas.

They brought us to a nearby school for shelter. Because Momma Hazel was pregnant again, the soldiers gave us privacy—a locker room to ourselves.

Yes, that's right. Hazel was expecting. AGAIN.

Hurricane Betsy would later be called "Billion-Dollar Betsy"—the first storm in U.S. history to cause over a billion dollars in damage. The levees broke on both sides of the Industrial Canal, including the one just across the street from our home. In Louisiana alone, it claimed the lives of seventy-five people.

I'm not sure how Tommy found us, the house was flooded and we were gone. His new car was filled with water. He saw Mr. Matthews on his rooftop with Bandit and some canned goods. Mr. Matthews didn't want to leave with the National Guard because his dog would've been left behind. Ms. Virginia had escaped just before the storm hit to stay with family. People could not go into their homes until the floodwater had receded. Tommy borrowed a canoe to assess the situation.

At some point, we moved into the newly built house on the "Best Bank" (a local slang for the "west bank"). I met a girl who lived across the street; her name was Renetta. She was my first friend, the same age as me. My very next friend was

Loa, and we did everything together. Her mom was one of our Girl Scout leaders, Ms. Joan.

Momma was meeting the neighbors too. Hazel liked to wow people with her "name." She wasn't usually a jokester, but she absolutely loved pulling this one out whenever someone asked what her name was: "Hazel Jane Mary Ann Suzie E. Bluebell Eliza Jean Sprinkins Johnson Sanchez."

A name she completely made up, it was a patchwork of wonderfully ridiculous hillbilly names that delighted people every time she said it.

Hazel tried her best to weave ordinary joys into the fabric of days. The Beatles sang from our crackling transistor radios, their voices tumbling through the air like secret promises of a bigger world. We baked cookies in our Easy-Bake oven, the glow of a single bulb transforming powdered mix into tiny little cakes and cookies, served proudly with frosted glasses of Tang—the drink of astronauts, though to us it felt like nectar from another planet.

We would go "make groceries" at Schwegmann's, the air inside cool and bright, aisles lined with treasures that seemed endless to a child's eyes. Some nights, if fortune was kind, we'd pile into the car and head for the drive-in (this is an out-door movie theater, for those of you to young to know). Fireflies flickered against the dusk as the giant screen came alive, casting its glow over the night.

Occasionally, we went to see the Mardi Gras fountain by the lakefront. I took piano lessons, my fingers stumbling across stiff ivory keys, while outside, the world was measured by the rising hum of cicadas and the specific rule that kids must be home before the lights came on —streetlights, those watchful guardians of childhood curfews back in the day.

Easter mornings found me and my sisters dressed in bonnets and little white gloves, our baskets filled with sugared treasures that glistened like jewels. And every December, Santa Claus never failed to find us. Stockings bulged, ribbons shimmered, and for a brief, breathless moment, our home glowed with the kind of magic that makes children believe the world is kinder than it is.

Hazel was the quiet seamstress of it all, stitching together rituals and small wonders, wrapping us in the gentle illusion of normalcy, as if love itself could disguise the rough edges of life.

We also went to Mardi-Gras every year. Momma would sew costumes for us all. We would usually start on Bourdon Street in the French Quarter and end the day at Grandma Long's house on Magazine Street.

Halloween was a big deal too, costumes and all.

Our family trips (vacation) were to "Pontchartrain Beach," an amusement park by the lakefront. We went once a year. Pontchartrain Beach in the 1960s and 70s was pure, bustling magic. Nestled along the shores of Lake Pontchartrain, it was the city's go-to amusement escape, a place where the heat of summer mixed with the salty breeze from the lake. Families strolled along the boardwalk, the scent of popcorn and cotton candy mingling with the lake air.

Ah, the Zephyr—Pontchartrain Beach's iconic wooden roller coaster—was the crown jewel of the park. It was a classic, built with a maze of timber tracks that rattled and groaned with every twist, drop, and turn. From a distance, you could hear the clatter of the wheels against the rails, a sound that was equal parts thrilling and terrifying, like a heartbeat you could see. The Zephyr wasn't just a ride; it was a test of courage. I remember this one time, up we went, slow and steady, the world stretching out below us. I could hear the creak of the timbers, the whine of the wheels, and the occasional shriek from a car ahead. Then—whoosh!—we plunged down the first drop, and my chest felt like it had been left behind at the top. My hands gripped the bar tight, knuckles white, hair whipping around my face as the Zephyr twisted and turned, dipping and soaring over itself. Every curve rattled me, every hill lifted me, and I laughed and screamed all at once.

One Halloween, our family turned the backyard into a haunted garden that was equal parts spooky and ridiculous—in the best way. Our neighborhood was filled with children from all over the area, their faces alight with excitement and a touch of terror. Morgus the Magnificent (my Dad) presided over the scene, complete with his beakers and test tubes bubbling with mysterious "potions." He was operating on my best friend, Loa, who screamed convincingly enough to make everyone pause. Hazel, dressed as a witch, stirred her brew like a pro, cackling at anyone who dared get too close.

The fountain was filled with hot ice and water, producing a wonderfully eerie fog that curled and twisted through the garden, making everything look like it belonged in a gothic horror movie—if that movie had a sense of humor. Guests tiptoed through the fog, half laughing, half terrified, never knowing if the next corner would bring a harmless prank or a scream-worthy surprise.

They would enter through the gate and dare to touch the "bowl of brains," which was really just a tangle of cold spaghetti noodles. Screams, squeals, and hesitant pokes made it feel terrifyingly real. Then, stumbling forward, they would collide with a hanging sheet of metal that clanged like thunder, jolting them as if the storm itself had struck. Between Morgus muttering ominously, Hazel cackling over her bubbling cauldron, the fog swirling around their feet, and the perfectly timed scares, the haunted garden was chaotic, creepy, and utterly unforgettable—a night where terror and laughter collided in the most magical way.

Hazel and Camille at new house 1966

New home under construction

Camille and Tommy (her daddy) 1966

I remember being told many times "We're your family, we raised you. Saving you from an orphanage." We would pass by the St. Vincent's Orphanage on Magazine Street in New Orleans weekly. It was just a few blocks from where Grandma Long lived, and the Antique Gallery was located. My parents would say to me "we saved you from that place. Orphans live there and they are made to peel potatoes all day until their fingers bleed." Another time they told me "If it hadn't been for us, you'd live in an orphanage. Your mother didn't want you."

Daddy Tommy, Becky, Camille & Baby Tina 1966

Those words burned through me, a pain I cannot describe. In my heart, I knew my momma Terri was a good person, because of the stories I was told about my brothers. She wanted them to be taken good care of while she was at Sara Mayo.

All was not well. In 1968, Hazel had another baby, lil Tommy. The responsibilities were becoming too overwhelming. Becky and Tina began their sibling rivalry, and baby Tommy constantly needed soothing, feeding, and changing. I was given "diaper duty"; she made it sound like a big opportunity…taking the cloth diapers and swishing them around in the toilet water until the poop came off, then you would need to flush the dirty water and put the diaper in a pail, proceed to the next one piled up with the dirties. I was in constant need, helping- helping- helping. While Momma Hazel was spiraling down deeper and deeper into the depression, she had no control over.

Depression is the emotional equivalent of drowning in quicksand.

At first, you might not even notice it, just a little heaviness, a slow drag beneath your feet. You tell yourself it's temporary. Manageable. But then the ground gives way, and before you can find your balance, you're already sinking.

Like quicksand, depression doesn't pull you under all at once. It's gradual. Quiet. You begin to feel stuck in place, unable to move forward, every small task requiring more strength than you have. The more you try to "snap out of it," the more defeated you feel, like struggling only sinks you deeper.

Your mind becomes muffled, as though wrapped in thick fog.

The world continues around you, bright and busy, but you're suspended in a heavy stillness— unseen, unheard. Panic may rise, but it finds no release. Hope seems distant, even naive.

Depression, like quicksand, begins to tell you that escape is impossible. The harder you try, the more you'll fail. But both, though cruel, can be survived. If you stop thrashing, if you reach for help, if someone reaches back, there's a way out.

Where do you turn to escape?

Chapter 6

How Did We Get Here

If you had asked Hazel, back in those days, if she was a Christian, she might've given you a blank stare and said, "I'm Catholic," with a kind of blank uncertainty, a vague shrug, as if the label alone was enough to satisfy the question. Deep down, though, she believed there was a God. That was certain. Not because someone had preached it into her but because somewhere in the shadows of her soul, she hoped there was something—someone—bigger than her pain. Her faith was more like an instinct, the kind of belief you cling to when you've run out of other options. It was quiet. But it was still there.

My father, too, had gone to Catholic school and mass. But if you pressed him, he wouldn't claim much of anything. Sometimes he'd talk about his own father, how he was an atheist, a mind wrapped in doubt and cynicism. He knew the rituals, but his connection to faith was even murkier.

And maybe that's where the silence came from, the silence in our house, the silence in our hearts. The kind of silence that doesn't come from peace, but from not knowing how to speak anymore.

Between 1965 and 1969, there's a strange fog in my memory—a stretch of years that live behind a veil I've never been able to lift. I've tried to peer into it, squinting through time like someone standing at the edge of a long hallway lined with closed doors, but there is no light slipping out from underneath them. No clues. Just shadow and stillness.

It's a time of complete darkness in my mind, without a glimmer of remembrance. That span of my life feels like someone tore those pages out of my book, pages that once held color. I've asked myself why I can't remember. Maybe it was too painful. Maybe my young heart tucked it away for safekeeping.

And then one day, I asked myself: How did we get here?

I had once been a joyful little girl, twirling barefoot on the porch, my dress catching the wind like a sail. I remember chasing butterflies through the backyard, the grass cool and wet beneath my feet, the sound of my parents' laughter coming from the kitchen window. The world felt kind then. Good kindness. My parents watched me with the kind of smiles that meant they believed in the goodness of the life they had started. There was a live oak in the backyard with long, stretching limbs I thought could touch heaven. Flowers bloomed along the stoop. Laughter echoed down the hallway. But it was beautiful. That was before the hurricane. Before things began to break apart, slowly at first, and then all at once.

I thought it would always be that way.

I guess my parents wondered the same thing: **how did we get here?** They had fallen in love with hope in their eyes and joy in their steps. Life was supposed to be better. But somewhere along the journey, that joy began to erode. That slow unraveling. That creeping feeling that what had once been whole was now slipping through their fingers. They had fallen in love the way all people hope to—eyes wide open, full of laughter, full of plans. Their wedding had been humble but bright with promise. They believed things would be better than what they had come from. That they would build something lasting.

Hurricane Betsy knocked out our lights, and our peace, with her wild, howling winds. Before my daddy started staying out later and later. Before the hush in my mama's voice turned into something quieter than silence. Before the weight of life pressed so hard on our house that even the walls seemed to sigh. Things didn't shatter all at once—they cracked. Subtle at first. Then faster.

By the time I was old enough to understand that something was wrong, the cracks had already spread. The air in the house felt different. Like it held its breath. My mother's face became sadder, as if joy had become something she kept tucked away for special occasions she wasn't sure would ever come. My daddy's laughter seemed to fade away, edged with something I couldn't name—maybe frustration, maybe guilt, perhaps just exhaustion.

I could still remember the days with dad waking up with a

song on his lips—belting out, "It ain't gonna rain no more, no more, it ain't gonna rain no more. How in the heck can I wash my neck if it ain't gonna rain no more?" Or he'd switch it up with a cheerful, "Yes, we have no bananas, we have no bananas today!" And if he wasn't singing, he was whistling—always whistling. Truth be told, he might've been the finest whistler in the whole South.

My parents were deep in one of their storytelling moods, diving into the lives they'd lived before they ever knew each other. My dad, with that mischievous twinkle in his eye, leaned in. "One night at the movies," he said, chuckling, "the orderlies had to carry out this young girl—screaming, kicking, the whole nine yards. It was absolute chaos. The smell of popcorn and disinfectant hung thick in the air, the screen flickering shadows across the walls, and all you could hear over the previews was her yelling shrill."

My mom froze, and said, "Wait, No way! That was me! She laughed, remembering the Mandeville Hospital field trip to Charity to have movie night with the teenagers from that hospital... let's just say I wasn't having a good time."

For a heartbeat, they just looked at each other, the absurdity sinking in. Two lives, on completely different paths, brushing against each other in a single wild, unforgettable moment. Fate, it seemed, had a wicked sense of humor—and a flair for irony.

Hazel wanted to be a good mother. She wanted to give her children a better life than she had known. But sometimes, in the deep hours of the night, she stared at the ceiling and felt the weight pressing on her chest. She was exhausted—not just from the work, but from the silence. From the loneliness. From the unspoken anguish she carried every day.

She was barely keeping it together. Four children, another

one growing inside her, and a husband who was more of a shadow than a partner most nights. Tommy was out late, working, maybe. Or maybe just escaping the weight of it all. There were bills, endless chores, teething babies, and constant noise. Hazel bore the burdens alone, and every day chipped a little more from her strength.

There were moments when she sat on the edge of the bed, tears running down her cheeks, rubbing her belly, wondering how she would go on. She missed her own mother, though they had never been close. She missed a version of life she had never even known, one with safety, with laughter that didn't fade, with a partner who deeply loved her.

Even though I was just a little girl, I could feel it all.

I was doing everything I could to help her with the kids, to keep her encouraged, to give her hugs. I knew she was relying on me. But I felt like I was failing. I felt like a child trying to hold the whole house together, and even then, I knew I wasn't strong enough.

Then, one memory broke through. Sharp, vivid, like it happened just the other day.

I was in fourth grade. And suddenly, there we were: me, Momma, pregnant with a brand-new baby, my cousin Donna, and Grandma Long, riding a steamboat along the Mississippi River beneath a brilliant blue sky.

It was one of those strange, bright memories that come uninvited but land with weight. I can still feel the wooden deck beneath my feet, still hear the paddlewheel thudding against the water, steady as a heartbeat.

There was a breeze that smelled like that old musty river and sunlight, and I remember how strange it felt to be out in the world with all four of us together. My mom had never planned anything like this before. I remember feeling a little out of place. Something about it felt off.

After lunch, Momma excused herself to go to the restroom. She was gone for a while. Donna, Grandma, and I sat at the table, sipping our tea and finishing our desserts. Then we heard it—a man yelling, "WOMAN OVERBOARD!" He yelled it several times, as people gathered around the bow of the ship to see what was going on.

I looked at Donna and Grandma and said, "That's my momma."

My heart knew. It just knew.

I had seen the days she couldn't get out of bed. The tear-soaked pillowcases. The bruises. I'd heard the fights and screaming late into the night. Sometimes I'd wondered how I was going to take care of my siblings if my Daddy killed Momma. These may not have been realistic fears, but the fears were real.

YES... it was her. She was the one overboard.

The boat came to a stop. A life ring had been thrown into the water, and a man managed to get her to the shore. I remember seeing her there, lying next to him on the riverbank. I watched from the deck in stunned silence. I wasn't sure if she was alive. I could barely take a breath; the wind had been knocked out of me. The questions were rolling through my head. Why would she leave us like this?

An ambulance came. They lifted her onto a gurney and drove away. Someone from the crew came and told us, "She's alive. They're taking her to the hospital."

I never got to see her while she was there. But I remember knowing—deeply—that the baby inside her was still kicking.

Still holding on.

Daddy came home early from work to be with us kids each night. He never said anything about what had happened. Not one word. Just silence. Heavy. Deafening.

The sound of silence was loud in that house—louder than yelling, louder than sobs. It filled the rooms, curled around the corners, and sank into the floorboards like damp air that never dried. At home, we kids felt the tremors of what we couldn't fully understand. There wasn't a name for the tension we lived in, but it had a shape—a sharp edge you learned to step around. The youngest ones, still toddling, clung a little tighter. My sister started wetting the bed again. My brother, usually so full of chatter, grew quiet. We all sensed it: something was unraveling. We tried to be good, to not cause extra trouble. We'd tiptoe when we used to run.

I was getting tired of trying to be strong. Now, we were experiencing a new kind of pain. When someone you love tries to commit suicide, the pain is not just about the loss of the person you love; it's about complete betrayal. Why do they want to leave us?

Of course, the person desperately trying to exit isn't thinking like that. They are just dealing with desperate cries for help, or truly desiring to get out of this world.

~ Selah ~ pause and reflect on this situation

Think about the impact on the tiny lives of her children.

I had already been dealing with a root of rejection because of being given away, and now I felt like my Momma Hazel had tried to abandon us. It's betrayal at the highest level.

Sometimes I would daydream of being with my birth mom, crawling up on her lap. Imagining what her hugs would feel like. Would she love me? Would she want to give me away again? Would she whisper to me, "You're going to be okay." Questions, just questions that couldn't be answered.

I never knew how long my mom was hospitalized; it felt like weeks, maybe it was days. Were the doctors treating her for mental problems or physical? I never found out.

All my daddy could manage to cook for us was scrambled eggs with canned diced potatoes. We ate that every night. I used to joke that if there was a casserole competition for

Depression food, he'd win second place... because no one would believe first place existed. But I had helped Momma enough in the kitchen to know the basics. So, I pulled up a chair to the stove and figured it out. Because someone had to.

Looking back now, I often wonder how Hazel was ever expected to survive, much less thrive. She had been released from psychiatric care as a teenager, just released. No follow-up, no ongoing treatment, no support network. Nothing.

It never made sense that the doctors believed she could handle life on her own, not at that age, and certainly not with her history. But I never asked why. Maybe it was because of our financial situation. Perhaps she was too young, or too old, for government assistance. Maybe no one wanted to deal with a girl who had been broken in the dark.

Whatever the reason, she was left to pick up the pieces herself. She lived with the depression, and I continued helping with the little ones as much as I could.

And still, she did it. For a while, she stitched those pieces together with thread made of sheer will. But there's only so much one heart can carry alone.

And that's how we got here.

A broken family in a broken house. A mother nearly lost. A child is trying to keep the walls from crumbling. A silence that spoke louder than words.

That's how we got here.

But this is not where the story ends.

Chapter 7

A Sacred Beginning

You never know when the journey is going to shift direction. It was an ordinary day in the life of a housewife, a mother moving through her routine like a tired tide: stopping quarrels, changing diapers, folding laundry, wiping counters, settling tantrums, and planning dinner. At that point, Hazel was nearly full-term with her new baby. I was nine years old. My baby sister Becky was five, Tina was four, and little Tommy was two.

Hazel moved through the chores of the day like someone wading through fog with busy hands, distracted thoughts.

She kept her eyes lowered, forcing herself to just make it to bedtime... one chore at a time, one hour at a time. She kept her eyes lowered; her heart focused on just one moment at a time.

Then came the next chore that changed everything: taking the trash can to the curb. She wrestled the heavy galvanized trash can down the driveway, scraping against the pavement. As she straightened up and brushed her hair from her face, she noticed our neighbor's son across the street.

There stood David, our neighborhood's very own Keith Partridge. He wore a short-sleeved, striped knit shirt in burnt orange and cream, tucked into a pair of faded corduroy pants with a leather belt. His sneakers had clearly logged more miles than some used cars, and his sun-streaked hair fell in those perfect, feathered layers that made him look like he was an all-American boy.

When he spotted Hazel, he called out, "Hey, Ms. Hazel! I got saved!"

She blinked at him, confused. "Saved from what?"

David paused - "You know... saved."

"No, I don't know," she replied, wiping her hands on her apron.

David fumbled. He wasn't sure how to explain what had happened in his heart, so he shrugged, waved awkwardly, turned to run off, and said, "I gotta go."

That strange little exchange hung in Hazel's mind like the smell of fresh-baked bread that lingers even after it's gone.

A few days later, Hazel saw David's mother, Ms. Joan, returning from school pickup. Joan was a "June Cleaver" kind of mom, she was always composed, always cheerful, the kind who remembered to pack napkins and make crafts for Girl Scouts. She was my troop leader and we adored her. (She could glue a macaroni wreath like a boss.) When it came to Artex embroidery paints, she worked like a pro, steady hands, and a patient heart. She was the Michelangelo of sweatshirts.

Hazel caught her before she went inside. "Hey, Joan, what did David mean the other day when he said he got saved? Was he in a fire? Did he nearly drown?"

Joan smiled, warm and knowing. She looked at Hazel's

puzzled face for a moment before replying, "He was saved from his sins, Hazel. That's what he meant."

Then she added, "I'd love for you to come with me to a Bible study. Just a small group. Nothing fancy."

Hazel hesitated. She didn't really know what a Bible study was. She had memories of stiff pews and cold stares. But something in Joan's voice made her nod yes. "Sure," she said, though she wasn't sure at all. "I'll get Camille to babysit the little ones. Can I ride with you?"

Well, that meeting changed everything.

At the gathering, Hazel learned about Jesus dying for her sins—not just a vague humanity, but for her. They spoke of grace, of a love that sought the lost. Of a Father who runs toward the wounded and weary. She kept going back, hungry for truth she'd never heard so plainly before.

Someone read from Revelation 21:8 and talked about spiritual death—about what it meant to be separated from God, not because He wanted it that way, but because we chose our own paths. Hazel thought about her own path— its sharp turns and painful cliffs. She thought about how she'd always believed in God, but never quite trusted Him.

Hazel's mom had taken her to the Catholic Church as a child. It rose before her like a towering stone fortress, majestic, immovable, and cold to the touch. Inside, the air was heavy with the scent of wax and dust, the quiet pressing against her like another wall. Sunlight filtered through the stained glass, casting fractured colors across the flagstone floor, but even the beauty felt distant, untouchable.

Hazel recalled her experiences. "The nuns who taught us seemed carved from the same stone as the church walls, unyielding, unbending, their faces lined more by severity than by smiles. Holiness, as they taught it, was an endless checklist you could never complete. There was a nun in class, and she kept a thick wooden ruler at her desk, not as a measuring tool, but as a weapon. The sting would fade, but the memory of her eyes, stern and harsh, never quite left me. And then there was the humiliation. Nothing quite burned like the heat that crept up my neck when the ruler cracked across my palm, the sharp sound echoing through the classroom. I could feel every pair of eyes on me, some wide with pity, others narrowed with relief that it wasn't them, and a few trying to smother their smirks behind cupped hands. I wanted to shrink, to disappear into the floor, to be anywhere but standing there with my throbbing hand outstretched like some criminal caught red-handed. It wasn't just the pain, it was being made a spectacle, the silent lesson to everyone else: this is what happens if you step out of line.

I believed in God's existence, but He seemed just as distant and stern as the ruler-wielding nun. I learned the rules, I memorized the prayers, but no one ever taught me to love Him. The Church gave me a spark of knowledge about God, yes, but it never fanned the flames. If anything, it made me afraid of getting close, because closeness might only mean more chances to fail. How could there not be a God? Look at the stars, the trees, the ocean. He had to be there. I just never thought He'd want anything to do with someone like me."

And then it happened.

It was like one of those long, relentless stretches of stormy weather, the kind that soaks the days and steals the light from every windowpane. After a while, you stop counting how many days it's been since you've seen the sun. Each morning began with the steady drumming of rain on the roof, a sound that at first was comforting, almost cozy, but eventually became a reminder that the sun was still in hiding. The rain becomes your rhythm. The air itself felt heavy, thick with the smell of wet earth and damp wood, clinging to your clothes and hair. Humidity feeling like the steam from a sauna. Streets turned into shallow rivers, reflecting a sky the color of pewter. Days like that begin to seep into your soul. You stop counting how many mornings have passed without the sun warming your face. You begin to feel that maybe it has forgotten you. The gray sky presses low on your spirit.

Just as the storm drenched streets and churned rivers, my days were soaked in tension, confusion, and longing. I trudged through them, careful not to slip on the slick memories that pooled beneath the surface. The wind whispered through the trees like voices I couldn't understand, and the thunder rolled with the rage and sorrow I often kept hidden. Even indoors, there was no escaping it, the storm mirrored the turbulence in our home, the chaos and unpredictability that shadowed my childhood.

Then one morning, without warning, you wake to find the storm has passed. The sun pours through the curtains like gold. The sky is a perfect stretch of blue. The air smells clean. You step outside, tilt your face toward the light, and inhale like it's the first real breath you've taken in months. There's no thunder, no drama—just quiet warmth. A deep and sacred relief.

That's what it felt like when Momma found faith.

Our little family had been weathering storms for years—some of them loud, some of them silent, some of them so deeply woven into our routines we didn't even notice they'd soaked through. But when Momma encountered Jesus in a way that felt personal and real—it was as if the whole house breathed out for the first time in years.

She accepted Christ at a home prayer meeting. And it wasn't just another prayer. It was the moment her soul was reborn.

Have you ever wished you could hit the reset button on your life—wipe away your mistakes and start again? That's precisely what happened to Hazel.

"Therefore, if any man be in Christ, he is a new creation: old things are passed away; behold, all things are become new."
—2 Corinthians 5:17

At first, the change showed up in her eyes. Then her countenance. Her face, once heavy with invisible burdens, began to lift. Slowly. Gently. There was a new lightness in her step. A softness in her smile.

And then—the singing started.

Let me tell you, Momma couldn't carry a tune in a bucket with two hands and a lid. The notes were so sour, they would make your ears pucker and remind you of fingernails on a chalkboard. But when she sang, it was pure joy itself. She'd hum in the kitchen while peeling potatoes, sing hymns while folding laundry, even belt out a line or two of "Victory in Jesus" while sweeping the porch. It was like someone had cracked a window in a musty house and fresh air rushed in.

She danced, too. Sometimes she'd grab a big kitchen spoon, hold it like a microphone, and twirl around like she was on the Hullabaloo TV show. We kids would laugh, and she'd laugh harder, saying, "If y'all only knew how good it feels to be free."

She taped scriptures to the fridge. She read her Bible in the morning, underlining verses and writing notes in the margins. She began to pray out loud—at the dinner table, before school, sometimes just while brushing our hair. There was no big ceremony to it. No fancy words. Just simple, heartfelt conversations with God.

And for the first time, I saw her truly see us. She wasn't distracted or weighed down. She looked us in the eyes when we talked. She touched our cheeks gently and said things like, "You're a gift, you know that?"

I had spent so long trying to be the strong one. Trying to hold everything together. But suddenly, I didn't have to anymore. I could breathe. I could be a child again.

It was during a time that would later be called the Jesus Movement. In the late 1960s and early '70s, a wave of spiritual revival swept across America. It wasn't led by preachers in suits but by barefoot dreamers in bell bottoms, young people tired of institutions, hungry for something real. They preached in coffeehouses, held Bible studies on the beach, and baptized strangers in lakes and swimming pools. Long-haired hippies with holey blue jeans would show up at the meetings and immediately get delivered from drugs. Then they would bring their friends, and the miracles became abundant. People were in awe of the events happening in their lives. Heaven came down and filled the air with grace, mercy, and love that was unimaginable. It was gritty and beautiful and raw.

And somehow, that Spirit made its way into our living room.

Hazel didn't need a revival tent or a choir. She just needed hope. And Jesus gave it to her.

The neighbors noticed. One of them said, "Hazel, something's different about you. You're glowing." She just laughed and said, "It's Jesus, baby."

She shared her story with anyone who asked—and some who didn't. She didn't sugarcoat it. She talked about the pain, the depression, the abuse, the darkness. But she also talked about grace. About how Jesus had reached into the pit and pulled her out.

She joined a church, started serving in little ways, and grew in her faith. She still had her flaws, still burned dinner from time to time, still lost her temper once in a while… but she had peace. Deep, abiding peace.

And our family began to heal.

We still had struggles. Daddy still carried his battles. Money was still tight. But there was a new foundation in our home— faith.

Not the kind that wears a mask or points fingers. But the kind that wraps arms around brokenness and says, "You're still welcome here."

That's how I remember that season. Not as perfect. But as sacred.

When I think back now, I don't just remember the hymns or the Bible verses taped to the fridge.

I remember her smile.

I remember how her laughter wrapped around our family like a blanket.

And I know, that was the beginning of something holy.

Chapter 8

Pathway through a Dream World

I was drawn to the scent of heaven itself, a rich bouquet of lavender, gardenias, and sweet magnolias that drifted through the air like a gentle song. The fragrance was so vivid, it felt as though the very breath of the garden was filling my lungs, wrapping around me like a soft shawl.

All around, colors bloomed in brilliant harmony, petals in hues of violet, blush pink, and creamy white swayed in the breeze. A golden light stretched across a serene lake nearby, its surface glowing like polished glass. Swans moved gracefully across the water, their white feathers catching the morning light as a delicate mist hovered low, turning everything into a dream wrapped in silk.

Drawn forward, I followed a stone path that curved through the garden like a whispered invitation. It led to a clearing, where long banquet tables stretched beneath a canopy of flowering trees. Each table was draped in crisp white linen, fluttering slightly in the breeze. Fine china rested at each place setting, trimmed in gold, and elegant candles flickered gently, casting a warm glow despite the daylight.

There was no noise, no chatter, only a deep sense of peace, like the world had been hushed to let the soul breathe. The place was filled with people I love and hold dear, some I hadn't seen in years, and others I had never met, yet somehow knew. And there she was, Momma Terri, radiant and peaceful, as if the years had melted away. Overhead, a grand pergola stretched across the banquet area, its beams wrapped in cascades of blooming wisteria, their lavender blossoms swaying gently in the breeze like nature's own chandelier.

All around me stood towering oaks, ancient and majestic,

their heavy branches cloaked in cascading Spanish moss that swayed gently in the breeze like silver lace. Birds sang from every direction, their melodies lifting through the trees like a celestial choir, soft and holy, as if the very air was humming with praise. Nearby, violinists played with quiet reverence, their notes mingling with the soft chords of a grand piano and the delicate strum of a harp, creating music that felt as if it had always existed. In the distance, the backdrop unfolded into rolling, snow-dusted mountains, timeless and serene.

I stepped closer to the flowering bushes, their petals opening like smiles, and there beyond them, a yearling grazed peacefully in a patch of sun-dappled grass—gentle, wild, and unafraid. A cool mist still lingered in the air, and through it, the morning sun streamed in radiant beams, piercing the branches of the old oaks with golden light that danced like blessings upon the forest floor.

Suddenly, a vivid blue butterfly fluttered past me, its wings catching the light like stained glass. It felt as though it whispered, "Good morning," as it drifted by. How could a moment feel so perfect, so weightless and whole? The air itself seemed to breathe love. Beauty shimmered in every corner, and music wove through it all like sunlight through silk. Everywhere I looked, faces glowed with joy. There were no burdens here, no shadows—only peace, only grace.

And then I realized... I wasn't awake. I was dreaming—yet the dream felt more real than anything I'd ever known. I had wandered into a realm beyond explanation, beyond reason, in a dreamland so intense...it was beyond comprehension.

 The years I spent in junior high felt almost like a dream—a season of rare light when our little family experienced a miracle. For about three years, transformation wrapped itself around our home like a quiet spiritual renewal rested over our household like a mantle of peace. Daddy began going to Church with us, Sunday after Sunday. He stopped drinking. The late nights at the bars became evenings spent at home, his presence steady instead of scattered. He became a deacon in that precious Church.

I remember one Sunday in particular. He stood up in front of the whole Church and sang a song. It was to the tune of Nat King Cole's Ramblin' Rose, but the words were his own: "Jesus knows, Jesus knows, all of my troubles, all of my woes. Why I love Him, why I serve Him—Jesus knows, my Jesus knows."

He didn't have a perfect voice, but he sang it from somewhere deep inside. And as the words filled the sanctuary. I remember fighting back tears because I saw a tenderness in my dad that I never knew existed. There was a gentleness in him that had always felt just out of reach. But in that moment, it was real. And it was beautiful.

The home Bible studies had grown so full that living rooms could no longer hold the people pouring in. What started as a handful of hungry souls gathering around coffee tables quickly became a movement too large to contain within four walls. So, a church was born, a place built with faith, sweat, and shared hope. They called it the West Bank Revival Center.

But it was more than just a church. It was the heartbeat of something sacred. We hadn't just found mercy and salvation—we'd found belonging. We discovered a spiritual family, people who not only prayed with you, but laughed with you, cried with you, and carried your burdens as if they were their own. There was a camaraderie there, a deep and unspoken bond forged through faith and shared experience.

It was as if God Himself had stitched our hearts together under one roof.

Some of my most cherished memories were made with those people. When I look back at that season of our lives, I know in my bones—it was the happiest time our family ever had.

The sanctuary filled with long-haired ex-hippies and former drug addicts, young seekers in tie-dye shirts and denim jackets, barefoot and searching. And oh, did they find something. One by one, they came in broken and left transformed. Many were instantly delivered from their addictions. It was like watching chains fall right before your eyes. There was a joy there—unspeakable joy—so real you could feel it vibrating through the air like music.

Wounded men were returning from Vietnam—haunted by war, limping with invisible scars—and somehow even they found rest here. In this place, they found hope again and a renewed strength that no battlefield could steal. There were tears, yes—but also healing. Deep, soul-level healing.

At the center of it all was our beloved pastor, Brother Reggie. He wasn't flashy or loud. He didn't need to be. He was a gentle soul, a man who radiated the love of God like sunlight. You couldn't imagine him saying a harsh word about anyone. He preached with kindness and lived with compassion. His voice was steady, his hugs warm, and his prayers powerful. Brother Reggie didn't just lead a congregation—he shepherded hearts. And in his lifetime, he reached thousands.

There was something unshakable about that place. A sense of unity, of grace, of radical love that surpassed denomination, background, and baggage. You could feel it the moment you walked in. People weren't judged for where they'd come from—they were embraced for who they were becoming. In a time when the world felt chaotic and divided, the West Bank Revival Center became a refuge for the weary and the wild-hearted.

The hippie culture—so often dismissed—had been crying out for truth beneath all the rebellion and color. They were searching for something real, something deeper than peace signs and protests. And somehow, miraculously, they were finding it. Right there, on the West Bank, under a steeple built from prayer and second chances.

The LSU Miracle

I was just a girl, maybe ten or eleven, and so was she.

I didn't know her name, only that her spirit was gentle, her smile soft and unafraid.

She was wheeled onto the stage— her body fragile, her limbs twisted. I didn't know at the time what was wrong with the sweet spirited soul, but now as I look back, I do believe she had muscular dystrophy.

It was a "healing service" being held on the college's campus. This girl was rolled up onto the stage in her wheelchair.

The minister began to pray. And then we all did— a hundred or more voices lifted like wings.

And then—something shifted.

Like the air itself bowed low, like time held its breath.

It was as if God leaned down and touched her.

Not just her body— but everything.

Her twisted limbs began to straighten right in front of our eyes. I was with my momma and Donna. We sat there in shock and bewildered as to what we were seeing right before our eyes. That young girl—that brave soul—began to rise.

As her arms and legs began unfolding, people on either side of her began to lift her out of the chair. She was able to stand on her own after about 10 minutes or so. People all around began shouting, clapping, and thanking God out loud for what they were witnessing. The air was electrified with excitement and energy; it was the most holy moment I had ever experienced. Then the unthinkable happened. She began to shuffle her feet and take tiny steps.

The joy upon her face was radiant, and soon her feet began to shuffle faster. Her legs had become completely straight, even though they were still thin and frail-looking. As she shuffled more with her tiny steps, she began smiling and clapping. The more she clapped, the more excited the ground became. I wondered if this was what it was like when Jesus walked this earth doing miracles; it had to be. After you see something like this in your life, I do think it must be terribly difficult to believe in your heart that God is not real. This experience, along with the miracle, transformed my momma's life and had an indelible impact on my soul for life.

I had gone from not remembering much of anything that had happened in elementary school to remembering so much that had occurred in the dream-like, marvelous years in middle school.

Some incredibly kind and gracious people from the West Bank Bible revival center paid for my way to go to a girls' camp in the summertime. It was amazing. Probably one of the best experiences of my young life, I had the opportunity to go to the same camp again the following summer. The camp was almost 3 weeks long. It was called Kueta-T in Zachary, Louisiana. It was a place of sunshine, horses, a swimming pool, good friends, great food, and a lot of love, singing, and laughter. I can still remember when the three weeks were up, crying because I didn't want to go home.

There were also two disturbing memories during those years. Even though my family had gone through so much healing, the people would sometimes revert to the old way of thinking and behavior.

One day, my daddy Tommy was in a rage. Someone had climbed up onto his chest of drawers; he knew "one of the kids" had done it. So, everyone was lined up for his rampage, around the edge of the bed. Spanking was the typical style of discipline in those times. Some parents held to the style of teaching a lesson. Another style was more brutal with a fierceness that damages the spirit of a young child.

That day, he was yelling at the top of his lungs, asking who did this. The dresser held a glass bowl and an antique vase that he treasured. It was broken, and he wanted to find out who had done this horrible act. I recall saying, "I didn't do it, Daddy." He paused for a moment and dismissed me to leave the room. My sisters Becky and Tina, along with little Tommy, were still lined up around the bed crying, each one saying that they did not do it.

As I was dismissed to leave, I encountered my mother standing outside the bedroom door, listening to the rage and beatings. She looked me in the eyes and asked one question. Calm. Cold. "Why are MY children being beaten and not you?!?" All I could say was that "I told him that I did not do it, and he believed me."

It was a moment too painful; I could not react, I stood there frozen. Her words cut through me to the deepest part of my core.

There seemed to be something there that caused her to treat me differently. A subtle coldness, a quiet distance. I was constantly introduced as "the adopted child".

I occasionally would think about how Terri went to Sara Mayo hospital to have me. And that Forrest and Keith stayed with Tommy and Hazel for several days. They took pictures of the brothers and really enjoyed the time they spent with them.

These were the pictures of brothers I didn't get to meet, I didn't get to know. Fortunately, I did get to hear the stories about them. For most of my life, I would hear about them. Keith and Forrest. Later, I would hear about another brother who was younger than me. Terri, who eventually went by Mariam, kept in touch with Tommy and Hazel. She eventually moved to California but would also make trips back to New Orleans for visits. She would stop at Tommy's antique store and inquire about me and how things were. They were also able to somewhat keep up with her life.

Years passed, and I remained very curious. However, when they told me their stories, they would also say things like, "We're your real family, we're the ones that raised you," "She gave you away," "She gave away her rights," and "You belong to us." This seems a bit like mixed messages, but I didn't really discuss it with anyone. I always had this feeling in the back of my mind that one day I would do my best to find them, although I didn't have a clue how. I know I've never even heard of anyone finding a family that they lost.

My Momma Hazel would recite words from a poem to me, "Not flesh of my flesh, nor bone of my bone, but still miraculously my own. Never forget for a single minute, you didn't grow under my heart but in it".

She told me many times throughout my life that I was the answer to her prayers.

But, there were nights when I lay awake, convinced I'd been

rejected, cast off, unwanted, left outside the circle of belonging. I often wondered if those feelings would ever loosen their grip. The song *"Creep"* always struck a raw chord with me. The song is a raw cry of human brokenness and the longing to belong. Its haunting melody and aching sense of not fitting in felt like someone had cracked open my own heart and turned it into music. If my childhood had a soundtrack, that song would have been the anthem—lonely, searching, and painfully honest about never quite belonging. So many times, I caught myself asking "why am I here?"

I learned not to talk about feelings because you never know if what you say might turn into a "mouth washing." One time, my father made me chew the soap, about half of the bar. I remember he kept saying, "OK, now get another bite." My Mom later got some toothpicks and tried to dig the soap out of the back teeth. Oh, what a night that was.

I do not recall my grandmothers ever hugging me. Their arms never opened to me; their words seldom found me. Was this because I was adopted? I don't know, as I was always afraid of what would happen if I asked.

Except for my great-grandma Long, she was different. Her kindness reached through the silence like the sunrise on a dark morning.

I had formed a beautiful friendship with a girl from the church. Her name is Helen, and she became my best friend, my big sister. I was maybe in 7th grade, and she was in college. Wow, she seemed so grown up; she drove a red Mustang convertible.

Camille & Helen - Early 70s

Her daddy had given her a credit card to a department store so she could go buy clothes and things. He would pay the bill. I had a deep respect for her dad; he was always kind to me. When Helen's sister got married (Kathy), someone mentioned to Helen, "Wow, the flowers at this wedding are some of the most beautiful I have ever seen." Helen replied, "Oh, my daddy grew these flowers." Well, later their dad was asked about his garden of flowers, and he later asked Helen why she would tell people that I grew those flowers, you know that I did not. Helen just smiled and said, "I was talking about my heavenly father, daddy". Helen could sing and write music, and she was also an artist. I think in many ways we had a kindred spirit.

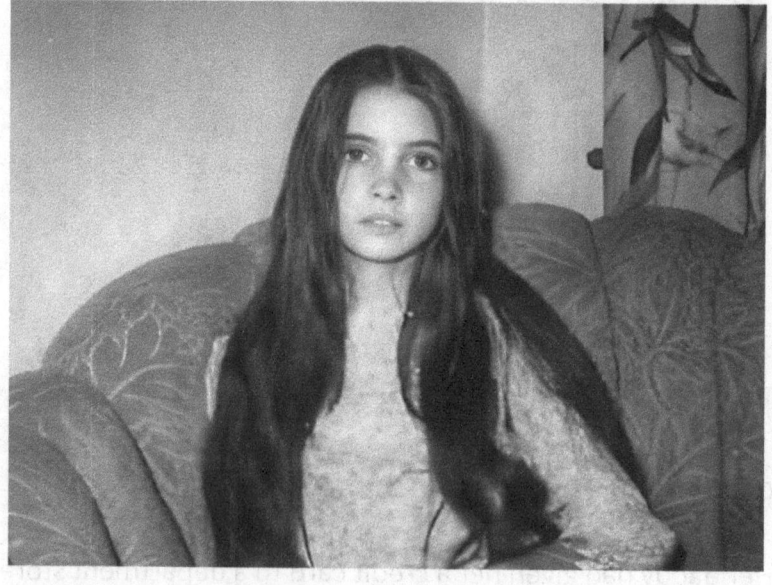

Camille - Photo by Helen Lingoni

The Haircut

My hair had grown long—so long that when I sat down, I'd have to sweep it to the side. If I forgot and leaned forward, I'd end up tugging it myself.

One evening, while Helen was over visiting, I decided it was time for a change. I asked my mom to trim my hair, just five or six inches, enough to make it easier to wash and manage.

Simple, really. A quiet moment, scissors in hand, hair falling like silk to the floor.

We got a barstool, the towel, the scissors, and everything ready. I went to the bathroom and wet my hair, came back and sat on the barstool. I put my hand in the middle of my back and asked my mom, Hazel, to cut it up to here. Then she took the scissors and took out a chunk of hair just below my right ear!

I asked her why she did it, but she didn't answer my question.

Her only reply was "now that I started here, I just have to finish it." Helen and I sat in shocking silence. When it was finished, I excused myself to bed and cried myself to sleep.

For weeks afterward, kids would approach me at school, wide-eyed and stunned.

"What did you do?!" they'd ask, as if something terrible had happened.

Then came the questions at church, at youth group, curious stares, whispered remarks, the same disbelief echoing everywhere I went.

It was awful... ugly, even. I was embarrassed by how I looked, but more than that, I was hurt. Deeply saddened that she had done this to me, as if my appearance didn't matter, as if I didn't matter.

Camille and Timmy

I wonder now, was I unknowingly adding to the weight my momma Hazel already carried?

Did the shadow of my biological mother stir something in her that made it harder to see me without seeing her?

There were always mixed messages.

"We love you like our own."

"God gave you to us—you were the answer to my prayers."

And yet, I would still hear those words echoed in my mind:

"Here's our adopted child, the one we saved from an orphanage."

And that question by the doorway, "Why weren't you beaten?"

And then there were the words I can never forget.

A family member, eyes sharp, voice cold:

"You're not our family. You were bought."

How do you unhear something like that? How do you unfeel it?

I knew, deep in my heart, that my Momma Terri loved me. I couldn't explain how I knew, I just did. There were no letters, no phone calls, but the knowing was there, steady and quiet, like a heartbeat beneath everything else.

As the years passed, I carried a dream inside me, a dream that one day, somehow, I would find her.

I didn't know how to begin, but the desire never left. It lived in me like a prayer I hadn't learned the words to.

Somewhere out there, I had a mother. A woman who had to

let me go. And I needed to find her. I had to find her.

Not just for answers, but for connection. For healing. There were puzzle pieces missing from my life, pieces scattered across time and memory, and I ached to gather them, to make sense of where I came from.

All my life, I lived with a quiet ache, a feeling that no matter where I was, I didn't belong, I didn't belong anywhere.

Not really.

Not yet.

Chapter 9

A Journey to the Edge of Sanity

Somewhere deep inside me, even as a child, I carried a quiet understanding— My parents were broken people. Not just flawed, but fractured in places I couldn't see, wounded by life, by their own pasts, by things they never spoke of.

They weren't the kind of broken you could fix.

They were the kind who lashed out when they were hurting, who loved imperfectly, who held their pain like a secret too heavy to share.

And somehow ... I knew.

I knew they needed love, not because they had earned it, but because they didn't know how to ask for it.

They needed forgiveness, not as a reward, but as a lifeline, as a chance to be seen, to be known, to be given what they never received themselves. They actually did pretty good considering the hand they were dealt.

It wasn't easy.

But I saw the ache behind their anger, the sorrow tucked inside their silence. And though they failed me in ways that still sting, I learned to love them from a place deeper than fairness— from mercy, from compassion, from a heart that understood brokenness because I had been touched by it too.

The Odd, Eventful Time

Things were already a bit unusual when I started high school. Girls attended one school, and boys were sent to another. I was in ninth grade. My school was far from home, so the bus arrived early (around 6:15 in the morning) to pick up students in my neighborhood. Classes started at 7:00 AM and let out by noon.

We were on what they called "the platoon system".

Half the students attended in the morning; the other half came in the afternoon.

It actually worked out well for me.

I loved those quiet hours at home before my younger siblings returned. I had time to read, to paint, to get lost in my thoughts or finish my homework without the whirlwind of little voices and chaos all around me. But that rhythm, my rhythm, wouldn't last.

It was sometime in the spring when things shifted. Strange rules suddenly appeared, out of nowhere. "You can't stay home by yourself," my mom said.

Tina, Timmy, Becky, Camille & Tommy

"If I have errands, you'll go to Ms Joan's house, or Miss Barbara's." I was confused. I'd always stayed home alone all the time. Why the sudden concern?

Then came more rules, and they were even stranger. "Don't answer the phone," she'd say sharply. "I'll answer it. Not you."

No explanation. Just tension. A sort of heaviness in the air I couldn't name.

Every day after school, I came home to new restrictions and my mother's guarded tone. No going out to play. No afternoon bike rides or weekend walks. Just stay in your room.

It went on like that for weeks. Whispers of something unspoken hung in the silence.

And then —just as suddenly as it began— it stopped. No warning, no conversation, no closure. Life returned to "normal," whatever that meant. But something had shifted in me. I never forgot that odd, eventful time, when the world didn't quite make sense, and I learned to pay attention to things that were never said out loud.

Loa, Tina, Camille, Timmy, Momma Hazel, Little Tommy, Dad, Becky

The Summer Everything Changed

Summer rolled around, and life finally felt normal again. No more strange rules, no more whispered phone calls. Just sunshine, youth group fun, and long afternoons with friends.

Best of all, camp was coming—Camp Keuta-T— a place that, to me, felt like heaven on earth. The pine trees, the songs, the late-night prayers, the smell of bonfires and bug spray. It was my sacred place: the three weeks out of the year when I felt totally free. No strife, no fighting, no stress.

But when camp ended that summer after ninth grade, I stepped out of that heavenly realm and straight into a plot twist I never saw coming.

My mom pulled up to pick me up. She smiled, popped the trunk, packed my things, and I climbed into the front seat, sun-kissed and full of stories I was dying to tell.

We'd barely pulled out of the parking lot when she said, "Oh, by the way... while you were at camp, we moved."

We. Moved.

Not across town. Not to another street. No. I mean moved!

From the West Bank of New Orleans to a speck on the map called McNeill, Mississippi. I say "map" loosely—I'm still not convinced that if you pulled out a paper map, unfolded it, that anyone could actually find McNeill on it.

I blinked. Surely this was a joke. But nope, my life had been packed up and relocated while I was roasting marshmallows and praising Jesus.

I never got to say goodbye to my friends. No final hugs at youth group, no last Sunday at the church I loved. Gone. Just like that. And to top it all off, calling anyone back home meant paying for a long-distance phone call, which, in our house, may as well have required a Congressional vote.

My safe little world— my neighborhood where I'd lived since kindergarten, where I could ride my bike to Brechtel Park, cruise over to the mall, or hop the city bus to downtown (alone, thank you very much). It was now just a memory.

In its place? Cows. Dirt roads. Farm smells. And a town where the only "mall" was a gas station that sometimes-sold nail polish.

This was my new home, it wasn't even on a real street; it was made of dirt! This was a place where you couldn't walk to church, you couldn't walk to a friend's house, and if you wanted to go anywhere, you better have a car.

I remember looking out the window as we drove those last country miles, thinking: What just happened to my life? I'd left for camp in one world... and come back to another.

That was culture shock! I'd lived on Morningside Drive since I was five, but suddenly everything felt new and jagged. In many ways, I was a typical teen: moody, offended by the world, always walking around simmering about something. My dad would bark, "Get that chip off your shoulder." The inner me wanted to place a chip there so badly — any chip would do, a wood chip, a potato chip — just something to sit on that shoulder. But my sense of humor wasn't seen as funny in that family. I knew he'd consider it disrespectful, and instead of a good laugh, there just might be a good beating. So I learned to keep the humor to myself.

She enrolled me in the local Podunk High School, and let me tell you, I loathed it with the fiery passion of a thousand suns. It felt like I had been ripped from the lively streets of New Orleans and plopped straight into an episode of the TV show Hee-Haw.

Before my tragic relocation to hillbilly land, there was a girl named Julia from my church back home. She worked at a hair salon in Metairie, and if memory serves, she might've been friends with Helen— they were close in age and shared that soft-spoken kindness.

Now, Julia had empathy, especially when she saw what that unfortunate haircut had done to my soul. It was less a hairstyle and more a cry for help. Without hesitation, she offered to fix it, for free. A gift from her heart (and from Jesus) I believe. I was stunned. Overwhelmed, even, by her kindness.

At the time, America was collectively obsessed with a darling little ice skater named Dorothy Hamill. She had that iconic wedge-cut bob—sleek, stylish, and cute. So, Julia, angel of hair salvation, decided I needed that haircut. She snipped and shaped, worked her magic, and voilà! Suddenly, I was sporting the Dorothy Hamill style, like magic.

Fast-forward to my dramatic entrance at the new high school in rural Mississippi, where I arrived looking like an Olympic hopeful stranded in tractor country.

Y'all. You'd have thought young Dorothy herself walked in.

Every flannel-clad bumpkin within a 20-foot radius turned

their head and took notice. A few of them "took a like'n", to this strange new girl with the famous haircut, big city talk, and just the right amount of "Who do y'all think you are?" in her walk.

It took time, and I mean a lot of time, for the anger to simmer down. This was not just the typical teen frustration; I was mad. Mad at my parents for uprooting my life without so much as a warning. Angry about being dropped in what felt like the witness protection program of high schools. And I made sure everyone knew it.

I'd march through the hallways, tossing out sarcastic questions like confetti: "Excuse me, where's the swimming pool?" "Do y'all not have tennis courts?" "Wait... hold up— no art department?! What kind of school doesn't let you paint your feelings!?"

Let's just say I wasn't exactly blending in.

Then came the day I got called to the principal's office. Me. Now, this was shocking. I wasn't the type to get in trouble, well... unless you count that one time, I stitched a full-on maze across the back of my hand with a needle and thread. A little performance art, if you will. My classmates were impressed. The teacher, not so much.

Anyway, I walked into the principal's office expecting a lecture, and that's **precisely** what I got, pep talk style. He leaned forward, all serious, and said something like: "Look... your parents aren't moving you back to New Orleans. So, you've got two choices: You can make the most of it here, or you can stay miserable. It's your call."

Ugh. I didn't want him to be the one making sense. But he wasn't wrong.

So—I took a deep breath, swallowed my sass (most of it), and decided to give this backwoods chapter a chance.

I tried out for the flag team—twirling like a Southern firecracker with something to prove—and made the cut. I dated a few guys here and there. Started a school newspaper because someone had to bring some culture to the place.

And somewhere in the middle of all that, I made a few real friends.

One of the brightest was Lori. I don't even remember what

drew me to her at first, maybe it was her infectious laugh, or the way she seemed to sparkle even when we were doing absolutely nothing. She had this way of making everything feel lighter. When I was with her, it was like all the heavy stuff faded away. Life didn't feel so hard. I smiled more. I laughed again.

And I started to believe that maybe, just maybe... there was still something good waiting for me here.

Even if it didn't come with tennis courts.

Back on the Home Front

Not long after my parents bought the country home, they decided it wasn't enough to just LIVE out in the sticks. No, they wanted to turn it into a full-fledged farm. And what does every farm apparently need? Cows. Which meant my very first initiation into rural life: a cattle auction.

I'll never forget walking in. I was about ready to have a "hissy-fit". The smell was like getting punched in the face by a compost pile that had been marinating in the July sun. It was manure, sweat, and something sour I couldn't place, it was like rotten milk mixed with wet dog. My parents seemed unfazed, as if this was the most natural place in the world to spend a Saturday. Meanwhile, I was trying to breathe through my mouth without gagging.

The cows were herded through narrow chutes, eyes rolling like they knew their fate, bawling so loud it rattled my insides. Calves cried for their mothers, and the mothers bellowed back. The whole place was a chorus of misery.

Then the auctioneer started. I swear, he wasn't speaking English. It was a rapid-fire chant, numbers blending into gibberish, like he was possessed by some hillbilly spirit, or a man having a stroke while speed-reading the phone book. I didn't understand a single word. "Habadabadaba—SOLD!" Every so often, a rancher in the crowd would twitch an eyebrow or flick a finger, and just like that, an entire cow was sold. My parents watched with the intensity of gamblers at a racetrack. They were beaming, soaking up the spectacle, while I was busy tiptoeing around puddles of mystery slime and praying none of it splashed on my shoes.

When the dust settled, my parents had bought cows. Actual cows. They were thrilled. Me? I just thought, YUCK—WE WILL ALL OFFICIALLY SMELL LIKE POOP FOREVER.

While I was adjusting to life in small-town Mississippi, things at home were unraveling fast. The younger kids were struggling—failing in school, fighting constantly. Tension hung in the air like the cigarette smoke.

Our dad's drinking had worsened. It was like watching a slow-motion collapse, and no one could stop it.

Daddy Tommy was a dangerous influence on my siblings. He had them drinking, smoking pot, sneaking into bars with him, and even getting caught up in crimes. I was never invited to any of it, not that it would have mattered. I was used to rejection.

Besides, I thought, if I have to do that stuff just to earn your love, I don't want it anyway.

But my siblings... they weren't so lucky. They craved his attention like a hunger that never seemed satisfied, starved for a father they didn't know how to reach. And so, they went along with him, following him down treacherous paths, doing things they knew were wrong, all for the chance at a connection, a fleeting approval. It almost destroyed them, and sometimes I wonder if the love they sought was worth the risk—but I also understand why they couldn't help themselves.

My mom stayed busy helping people, so I'm not sure how much she realized about what was happening. As for me, I kept myself occupied with school, work, and other things, carving out a space where I could stay out of harm's way and just survive.

During those few years in the country, I came to realize that our family had developed a reputation. Whispers in town, sideways glances, like people already knew the storm that lived inside our walls.

It felt like we were living out Matthew 12:45— evil returning, seven times worse than before.

One memory still burns bright in my mind. The day I saw my mom getting beaten. Something in me snapped. I have had enough, I thought. It was like the proverbial last straw. A fury I didn't know I had rose up inside me. I raced up the stairs, looked him dead in the eyes, and screamed, "STOP IT! Or I will call the cops!"

I meant it. And he knew it. He never laid a hand on her again.

Hazel

Somehow, through all the wreckage, my mother found a way to fight back—not just for herself, but for others too. This also helped her escape from the hell at home.

She started a shelter for abused women. She rented a modest house, got backing from United Way, and began building something sacred from the ashes of her own pain.

She called it The Agape Women's Shelter— Agape, meaning "God's Unconditional Love". The kind she wished she had received.

The kind she gave to others, even when she was running on empty. Churches stepped in to help. Donations came.

And my mom?
She poured every piece of her heart into that place.

Because she knew what it meant to be trapped. What it felt like to live in fear. And what it took to escape. She turned her own suffering into a sanctuary for others. And to me, that was the bravest thing she ever did.

Chapter 10

Hope on a Half-Tank of Gas

In my senior year, my dad surprised me with a "real gem" of a car: a 1960 Volkswagen station wagon that had clearly been in a demolition derby, or at least lost one. "It's a great deal," he said, "only a hundred bucks!" The hood didn't latch, so I had to keep it tied down with rope, because if it flew up while I was driving (and it did a couple times), I'd be staring into the underbelly of the beast with zero view of the road. But believe it or not, I loved that busted-up little car. It gave me a taste of freedom, and I laughed every time it rattled to life like a dying lawnmower.

With my newfound mobility, I got a job and started driving to a church an hour away in Hattiesburg, "The Storehouse". That place was like breath for my soul. Brother Matheny, the pastor, had once been a missionary to Kenya with his family. I remembered him from the Westbank Revival Center, where he and his family used to visit when they were stateside. I honestly don't remember how I reconnected with his church (this was pre-internet, pre-social-media-anything) maybe through one of Momma's old friends or a church newsletter mailed to our house. However, it happened, it felt divinely timed. The people there were kind, welcoming, and treated me like I belonged.

Meanwhile, I was trying to keep my head above water. I just wanted to finish high school, go to college, and escape the chaos. After getting my little tin can of a car, I got a clerical job during the day and picked up a waitressing shift at night. I was out of school by 11 a.m. (not many credits left), worked the office till 5, then slung food from 6 to 10. Go home, sleep, and hit repeat.

One day, my senior English teacher, Ms. Massey, pulled me aside after class. She looked me in the eye and said, "I know things aren't good for you at home. You have to go to college. There are grants that could pay for it." My heart leapt. I raced home, bursting with hope, and told my parents. "I could be an architect! or become a college professor in a great art department! I could do something, anything!"

Their reply? A heartbreaking, soul-stomping NO! They told me how my dad had never paid income taxes. He forged paperwork just to buy a home, and if I filled out the applications with his name, he'd go to jail. "Is that what you want?" they asked. "You wanna put your own father in prison?!"

Then came the Army recruiter. Everyone at school took the placement test, and I apparently knocked it out of the park. (Maybe they tell everyone that.) He told me that if I joined up for just a few years, all my college would be paid for. I took that idea home, too... hope round two.

This time, the response was more colorful: "Hell no, there's no way we're letting you do that. Not no way, not no how!"

I was stuck. I was blocked at the end of a dead-end street. My journey is full of potholes and roadblocks, and I was becoming more than discouraged.

Near the end of the year, I finally confided in Ms. Massey and her husband, Coach Massey. I told them everything. I still don't understand how they had the capacity to care about me, Ms. Massey was fighting cancer, they had two small kids, both worked full time, and lived in a mobile home parked on school grounds. But they saw me, and cared about me and my situation. They invited me over for dinner one night. Ms. Massey took my hand and said, "Sweetheart, you can go to college. You don't have to use your father's name. We can help you apply as an independent. But to do that, you'll need to leave that house. You can come live with us."

I cried like someone had opened a dam. For the first time, I saw a way out. My dream roared back to life: I'll go to college, get a good job, I'll find my birth family and Momma Terri, and everything will finally make sense.

But of course, you can probably guess what my parents said.

NO. Again. And again. And again.

Even my coworkers at the Army clerical office saw something was wrong, though I never told them. Maybe it was written all over my face. That job was part of a student worker program, and if I wasn't enrolled in school after graduation, I'd lose it.

Two engineers I worked with decided to open a private office and asked me to run it. I was floored. A plan was forming: I'd go to junior college for drafting, work in the afternoons, pay my own way, and finally stand on my own two feet.

I got a student loan for the first school year, attended school in the morning, and worked afternoons. It was hard. My little VW car needed a quart of oil every day, so most of my paycheck went to gas, food, and oil just to keep the thing coughing down the road.

Then my dad had a "great opportunity" for me.

He said silver prices were skyrocketing and that if I gave him the rest of my school loan money I had saved, he could double it. I didn't feel too good about doing that, but he assured me that he knew what he was doing. So, I withdrew the money and gave it to him.

When the next semester came around, I asked my dad for the money. He said, "the money is gone. I needed it to pay a gambling debt," he said, like it was nothing.

Gone—like my things he sold. Gone—like Mama's wedding ring. Gone—like my dreams.

I had to drop out. I couldn't afford to keep going, and now I had a loan to repay with no degree to show for it. The only light in the mess was that the engineers went ahead, opened their new office, brought me on board. That gave me work and dignity.

During that season, I leaned on my friends at The Storehouse. My faith community kept me afloat. My dear friend Nancy became my anchor. I often stayed at her family's house on weekends.

Nancy's encouragement comes not as empty words, but as a force that breathes courage into my bones. Compassion is woven into her very being; she sees hurt before it's spoken and responds with a tenderness that disarms sorrow. Yet within her gentleness burns a warrior spirit, fierce and unyielding. She leads not with arrogance, but with conviction, moving through life with a vitality that demands both respect and admiration. Beside her, I am reminded that strength can be kind, that victory can be graceful, and that love—unyielding, courageous love—can conquer more than fear ever could.

Sometimes, after Sunday lunch, I'd head straight to Slidell. My new office was a godsend, I could sleep there to save gas money. It was upstairs from a bank, sparkling clean, with French doors that opened onto a little balcony and a private bathroom. Home enough, even though it was a pallet on the floor.

Because let's be honest, if I went back home, there'd be dirty dishes stacked to the ceiling, someone yelling, and more of the same heartache.

So, I stayed. I worked. I pressed forward.

And I survived.

Chapter 11

Detours Toward Belonging

There's no telling where the road will take you when you don't have a map, or even a clear sense of where you're going. The path I thought I was on had been bulldozed. My carefully laid plans: college, a future in architecture or the arts, a fresh start. These were swept away before I even had the chance.

Looking back, I realize something that never occurred to me then: I could have chosen another way to rebel. I could've said yes to Ms. Massey and her husband when they opened their home and offered me a lifeline. I could have packed a bag, walked out, and carved my own path. But it never even crossed my mind.

I wasn't wired that way. I'd always been the compliant one, the rule-follower, the quiet observer who never wanted to make waves. Rebellion wasn't in my nature. I saw it all around me, in friends, family, in movies, in music, but I didn't yet see it as a lifeline, or a form of survival. I thought being "good" meant obeying, even if it led me straight into heartbreak.

And so, I stayed and obeyed. Not because I wanted to, but because I didn't yet know I had a choice. I am not sure if I stayed out of duty, out of fear, or out of the tangled idea that sacrifice equaled goodness.

But even in that choice, reluctant as it was, something unexpected unfolded. A quiet twist of fate.

One Sunday morning at Storehouse Church, I heard about a Christian concert coming up at William Carey College, David Meece was playing, and I loved his music. I scraped together enough to get tickets for my sisters and me, and we were excited to have a night out together.

When our neighbor Marie heard we were going, she asked if I could grab two extra tickets, for her and a friend. I didn't think twice.

The night of the concert came, and we found great seats near the front of the auditorium. Marie and her friend, David, came over to say hello before the music started. He seemed kind. Friendly. Nothing particularly remarkable... yet.

I casually invited them to join us afterward at Sebastian's, a cozy little restaurant my friends and I liked to go to after church events. It was just a quick invitation, nothing fancy. But life has a way of taking ordinary moments and threading them into something else.

I didn't know it then, but that night was the beginning of something entirely new.

David and I had what I'd call a mildly forgettable conversation that night at the concert, one of those polite exchanges about jobs and hometowns. I mentioned I worked out of an office in Slidell, and he casually said, "Oh, really? I grew up there."

"Where's your office?" he asked.

"Gause Boulevard—upstairs in the new bank building."

My little Office - Gause Blvd., Slidell

We chatted a little more... the usual small talk. Bla bla bla. I honestly didn't think twice about it.

A few weeks later, I was at work when I heard a knock on the office door. That was odd, people didn't usually come to me. I went to them. I hesitated to answer it since I wasn't expecting anyone. No appointment. No heads-up.

I cracked the door open and there he was— a vaguely familiar face, smiling. David. (Though, for the life of me, I couldn't quite place where I'd seen him before.)

He "just happened" to be in the neighborhood. "Just happened" to remember where I worked. And "just happened" to stop by... to ask me to lunch.

Subtle, right?

We could take the scenic route through the backroads and highways of the next ten years, but I'll give you the Cliff Notes version: Dave and I hit it off. We shared more than a few things in common, including a deep love for God, who had somehow shepherded us both through some hard, messy chapters.

Dave's the kind of guy who naturally takes the reins the moment he walks into a room. Leadership isn't something he strives for, it just flows out of him, like gravity pulling everything into its rightful place. He loves to keep things light with a well-timed joke, disarming tension with humor that makes people feel at ease. Between his Cajun-accented Boudreaux and Thibodeaux jokes and the way he can make a story come alive with every twist of his accent, you're guaranteed to be laughing long before the punchline hits.

Beneath the wit, though, is a steady core of faith that grounds his strength. He thrives on helping others, often stepping into situations like a modern-day superhero, eager to lift burdens. Some admire him for the confidence he carries, while others appreciate how he makes them feel safe in his orbit. He has a way of making people believe that no matter how high the waves rise, he'll find a way to steer the ship to safety (or get killed trying).

Wedding Picture with Family 1981

Dave had his share of hardships growing up, but he hasn't let them break him. Instead, they've shaped him into the man he is today—resilient, funny, loving. When we were newly married, we made a promise to each other: if we ever had children, we would do our best to give them a better life than we had.

He can grill better than anyone I know: steaks, shrimp, ribs, you name it, he'll make it sing. if there were a world championship for perfectly charred steaks or smoky chicken, he'd be bringing home the gold.

In time, we got married and were blessed with a remarkable little boy named Benjamin. From the very beginning, there was something extraordinary about him. I wasn't new to caring for kids, I'd practically raised my younger siblings, did plenty of hours babysitting, and worked in more nurseries than I could count. I understood children. I knew their habits, their ways, and all about those tantrums.

But nothing could have prepared me for the tidal wave of love that hit when I held my own child. Ben was an amazing little boy. He was the kind of boy who filled a room without meaning to—lively, curious, a spark darting from one thought to the next. His eyes were always wide, not with mischief alone, but with wonder, like every object in the world was holding a secret waiting to be solved. Strong-willed, yes. He would argue the sky was green if only to prove he had thought it through. But he was so lovable, you couldn't stay frustrated for long.

He took things apart just to see how they worked, sometimes forgetting to put them back together. He tucked little treasures away in his room—matchbox cars hidden under pillows, half a sandwich wrapped carefully in napkins and slid behind a stack of books, a marble or two under his bed. It wasn't about hoarding; it was his way of keeping the world close, keeping pieces of it to study, to marvel at again when no one was watching. He was experimenting, pushing, and collecting knowledge in the way other children collected toys.

He was all energy and wonder, the kind of boy who couldn't help but study the world like it held puzzles meant just for him. Constantly tugging at the seams of things, always asking why and how, always testing if rules were really rules or just suggestions.

His curiosity had no limits, and neither did his inventions. I'll never forget the day I walked into his room and found that he had spun a spider web—literally. He'd taken an entire roll of dental floss and strung it from wall to wall, dresser to doorknob, headboard to closet. You couldn't step inside without getting tangled. Part of me wanted to scold him, but the bigger part just marveled at his creativity. He didn't do anything halfway—if he imagined a spider web, then by God, he was going to build one.

When Benjamin would look up at me with those big, trusting eyes and say, "Mommy, I love you"—I swear, my heart didn't just melt. It puddled right onto the floor.

See, I really can't write this book without writing about my own family. They are the heart and center of everything in my life.

A few years later, we were given a second miracle: a daughter, Bethany. She came into the world like a little cherub, with the bluest eyes I'd ever seen, eyes that saw straight through me. And the love she brought pierced through every cracked corner of my world, like light spilling through stained glass. It cut across the rough edges, filling the hollow places I thought would never be filled. It was like sunlight, scattering color and warmth across even the darkest parts of me. I had thought I understood love before her, but Bethany deepened the meaning. She was laughter bottled up in the body of a baby, music disguised as a heartbeat, a promise I never dared to dream I would be given. Even now, words fall short when I try to describe it. All I know is this: she transformed me. Utterly. Forever.

Bethany was a little angel, her defiance always sweet. Imagine a two-year-old, her softest, gentlest voice barely above a whisper, saying, "NO, Mommy," and somehow melting your heart all at once. She had a tender spirit and a love for animals and everyone she met. It was rare to see her angry, unless a sibling pushed just a few too many of her buttons.

From the earliest days, she showed an eye for beauty and a quiet appreciation for artful things, traits that continue to touch me even now.

And, oh, how Ben fell in love with her. From the very first day, he was stricken, completely captivated, as if this tiny bundle had cast some sort of spell over him. He'd kiss her and hug her relentlessly, smothering her with a kind of brotherly devotion that sometimes made me laugh and sometimes made me gently pry him off so she could breathe.

Wherever we went, Ben turned into her self-appointed spokesman. At the grocery store, in the church foyer, even in the checkout line at Walmart, he'd tug on a stranger's sleeve just to beam with pride and announce, "This is my sister, Bethany!" as though she were royalty and he, her herald. People couldn't help but smile at his enthusiasm, he made sure Bethany's entrance into the world was celebrated far and wide.

The two of them grew into the best of buddies. Their laughter ricocheted through the house like music, their secret games and made-up adventures creating a world all their own. Their love for each other shone brighter than any sunset I've ever seen, fierce and unshakable. They could squabble like any siblings, sure. but even in their disagreements, there was a tenderness, an invisible thread tying them together.

Sometimes I wondered if God had tucked a little extra glue

into their bond, the kind that couldn't be undone. Watching them together was like watching a living parable of loyalty and joy—an unspoken promise that neither of them would ever be truly alone in this world.

Bethany noticed details that no one else did. I remember one afternoon, when she was a teenager, rushing to the car after a grocery run, thinking she was lagging behind. When I looked back, there she was, kneeling beside a man in a wheelchair, helping him with his grocery bags. That was Bethany, thoughtful, observant, and compassionate beyond her years.

As I watched these two little ones grow, my thoughts wandered back, again and again, to Forrest, Keith, and Momma Hazel, watching over them in the recesses of memory. I carried those figures with me like half-remembered dreams, polishing them with imagination until they gleamed brighter than reality ever had. Maybe I daydreamed about that family more than I should have, but how could I not? They were the unfinished chapter, the echo in a song cut short. They were the missing pieces, the unanswered verses in my story. I wouldn't call it an obsession, but I knew with a certainty deep in my bones: the questions would never loosen their grip on me until I sought the truth for myself.

And beneath it all pulsed a quiet unease, a whisper I couldn't ignore, that when the answers finally surfaced, it would change everything.

I had a dear friend who helped me study for a flight attendant position with an airline. I was overjoyed at the thought, this was going to be AWESOME. I pictured myself soaring through the skies, flying like the angels. Okay, maybe not EXACTLY like the angels, but close enough. At the very least, I'd have those dreamy travel perks, and when I found my Terri, we could visit all the time.

I studied diligently, memorizing safety protocols and service scripts like they were gospel. I dressed in my most prestigious, "ready-for-takeoff" outfit and walked into the interview process with confidence buzzing through my veins. I felt it in my bones—I had done exceptionally well.

At the end, the spokesperson assured us that all eligible applicants would receive a call on a specific date to let us know if we qualified. So I waited by my faithful landline phone all day long. I didn't leave for a moment. Not even to run to the corner store for milk. That phone and I became one entity—I was READY.

But the call never came. I waited, and waited... and nothing. By nightfall, I was in tears. It had seemed like the perfect job for a young mom: only three days away from home each week, steady pay, and the thrill of adventure. But it wasn't meant to be.

And then, as life often does, it surprised me in a way I never could have imagined. The following week, I found out we had another little miracle growing inside me. A different kind of flight path. One that would keep me grounded, yes—but also lift me higher than I'd ever thought possible.

This time, I was a bit nervous. Dave was buried in schoolwork and exams, stretched thin and worn down. In many ways, I felt like a single mom, doing all the day-to-day on my own. The thought of adding another baby to the mix felt completely overwhelming. Could I really do this?

But then my mind would drift to my momma Terri, and the impossible choice she made to give me up. And I knew, deep in my bones, that I could never do the same. I loved my two children with every fiber of my being, and no matter how hard this road might get, I would love this third child just as fiercely.

Even if it meant late nights, harder days, and carrying more than I thought I could—I would do it. We'd find a way through. Dave would finish school. Life would get steady. We'd be tired, maybe. But we'd be okay. We'd be a family. And love, somehow, would be enough.

I never really had the option of letting the kids spend the night away with family. There were things with them that scared me as a mom. I never felt safe leaving them.

Here's a bridge, rickety and trembling, groaning under its own weight. It asks nothing of you—except to stay away. We shall not cross it. On the other side lies a murky swamp where darkness sits heavy, curling around every root like a living thing. It's covered in poisonous snakes, and even the air itself seems to breathe venom. And the wind carries whispers you do not want to hear.

Here, you'll find people with hearts as black as coal, carrying their cruelty like a shadow stitched to their souls. There are monsters here—some don't growl; they smile and ask how your day's been.

This place has seen horrors no one wants to speak of. I will say, that some of the things that happened in this horrendous habitation was cruelty, drugs, innocence lost, there are dysfunctional families, where children are beaten until they bleed, where a sibling grabs piece of lumber to try to slam it like a bat into their dad's head, where a dad teaches his kids to become addicted to drugs and alcohol...and have his sons serve time in jail for the horrific things he's taught them, souls stolen, prisons that tried to bring justice, and even the youth vanished into the reeds without a sound, murdered. The swamp remembers everything, the sins, the silence that follows. Someday... it would later become a place of grace, but for now, we will detour around this place.

In the summer of 1990, we were living in Dallas and had made the long drive back to Mississippi to visit family. My parents were divorced by then. Mom had settled into a small house in Picayune and was still pouring her heart into running the women's shelter. Dad would usually drop by briefly when he heard we were in town—never staying long. He'd say something random like, "How 'bout them Cowboys?" then quickly make an excuse to leave— "Gotta grab cigarettes," or some other convenient exit.

During that visit, something unexpected happened. My mom's friend Jane quietly came into the guest room one afternoon while I was folding clothes. She sat on the edge of the bed and said, "Camille, I want to tell you something. I found a group that helps people locate their birth families.... Do you want to find yours?"

Her words hit me like a lightning bolt: clear, sudden, and electric. Impossible to ignore. I nodded slowly and said, "Yes. More than anything." Then I lowered my voice and added, "But please, don't tell my mom. Just send me the information. Here's my address in Dallas." Jane promised she would.

I thought about what she said and the possibilities of finding them. I felt there was a void and emptiness in my life. The stories of my lost family helped some, but they were only bits and pieces of a puzzle (the puzzle of my life), which had so many missing pieces. I had been given facts and information, but because there was no memory of this past, I had empty spaces in my heart, empty, empty places crying out to be filled. I felt as though I was expected to regard my birth family as dead, non-existent - if not literally, then symbolically.

The next night, after I'd tucked Ben and Bethany into bed and sat down for what felt like my first breath in twelve hours, my mom appeared in the doorway, with fire in her eyes, voice sharp as a switch. I'm pretty sure that was the onset of a full-blown conniption fit.

"What's this I hear about you wanting to find your birth family, but you don't want me to know about it?!?!"

In my head, I screamed, Jane, you traitor! But it was too late.

What followed was not a conversation. It was a three-hour emotional tug-of-war. There were tears, raised voices, and years of unspoken pain on both sides. I tried to explain: "I'm not replacing you. I'm not rejecting you. I just want to know who they are. They're part of me too. Can't you see that?"

Mom, you tell me stories about Keith and Forrest, and how cute baby Chris was with his bed inside a dresser drawer. You want me to know about them. You took pictures to give to me, but they were destroyed in hurricane Betsy. Then you say things like, "Why do you want to find them? What kind of mixed-messages are you trying to send to me?"

I told her, "People have stepfamilies all the time, stepmoms, stepdads, half-siblings, and they learn to love everyone. Why can't you believe I have room in my heart for both?"

But she only responded with the same old refrain: "We're your real family. We raised you. We saved you. She didn't want you." And in that moment, I realized—this wasn't just about me finding someone. It was about her fear of losing me. Even if she didn't know how to say it.

Then I told her, "Mom, I am almost 30 years old, I am married, I have two children and one on the way. I think I am old enough to finally know who my family is."

Then she gave me enough information for me to begin my

search. She said their names are "Terri, Teresa Halter, Keith and Forrest, Chris or Christopher, and Jennifer or Jessica Halter. Your mom was from Minnesota and moved to California when the boys were little."

And then she said something that took my breath away: "Your birth mom has wanted to meet you for years. She's come to New Orleans several times asking about you."

She wanted to know me.

She'd never stopped wanting me.

And with that, the search began—not just for them, but for the missing pieces of me.

Chapter 12

Exit 1991: The Way Home

When we arrived home, I began my search. Our new baby was due to be born in September, so I had some time to work on my search before I would get crazy busy with a newborn. With my list of names in hand, I began by making phone calls. I would call "information" 411 in Minnesota and California. I would get the number for any "Halter" people in the area. Once I received a phone number, I would make the long-distance call. Because phone calls could get expensive and we were on a student's budget, I would do my best to keep them short.

My intro into the calls "Hi, I'm Camille, I grew up in New Orleans. I am doing some genealogy research. Can you tell me if you know any of these people: Terri. Teresa Halter. Keith. Forrest. Chris or Christopher. Jennifer or Jessica Halter."

Many nights after the kids were in bed, I would make these calls, looking, searching, but not finding. Dave came home from school one day and said that he heard that the Mormon church in our area had extensive genealogy records. I contacted the Mormon church, and they were not able to help me either. I didn't know of another way except to hire a detective, but I knew that we couldn't afford that. So, I continued to make the phone calls.

Then the plan goes on hold.

Middle-of-the-Night Mayhem (a.k.a. Back Labor and a Racer's High) It's 1:00 AM and my back is staging a full-blown mutiny. I shuffle to the living room like an elderly penguin and collapse onto the sofa, hoping for relief. During my pregnancy, I found out I have scoliosis—because why not add a plot twist to an already dramatic third trimester?

I've developed a genius (or desperate) little trick: remove

one sofa cushion to create a belly-sized dip, then drape myself over the gap like a weary walrus, with extra pillows supporting the rest of me. It's not elegant, but it beats trying to sleep on a spine shaped like a question mark.

1:30 AM rolls around. My clever cushion hack isn't cutting it anymore. I doze off for a few precious minutes, only to be jolted awake by a deep, gnawing pain in my lower back. The kind of pain that makes you question every life choice that led you to this point.

By 2:00 AM, the pain has gone from "ouch" to "IS THIS HOW I DIE?" It finally dawns on me—oh. I'm in labor. Back LABOR! Fantastic.

I stumble to the bedroom and wake my sweet husband: "Dave. Dave. Wake up." He bolts upright, groggy and alarmed. "WHY?" "We're having a baby." "Oh."

Cue instant chaos.

Dave springs into action like he's on a reality TV show. He gets Ben and Bethany out of bed, starts throwing clothes and snacks into bags like a dad on a mission. I'm waddling around the house between contractions, trying to find ChapStick and baby clothes, and maybe remaining poised.

We drop the kids off at a friend's house and head toward the hospital in downtown Dallas. Now, here's where things get really crazy: Dave is driving like he's in 'The Cannonball Run" movie. He's grinning, cruising the highway like he's Mario Andretti, meanwhile I'm in the passenger seat trying not to scream every time we hit a bump, and feeling like someone has slammed my back with a sledgehammer. I tell him to slow down... If he tells me we're "making great time." I will punch him.

We pull into the hospital parking lot at exactly 5:00 a.m.

At 5:05, our Sweet Baby Rae is born.

Five. Yes, five. Minutes. Later. No epidural. No time for questions, and there she was—our fierce little boss babe, announcing herself with lungs full of purpose.

This girl was ready. And clearly, this girl knows how to make an entrance.

Memaw Hazel comes for a visit. Mom decided to come stay with us in Dallas for a few days—to help with the baby and, you know, do all the magical grandma things.

One quiet evening, she was rocking baby Rachael in the big blue recliner. The room felt comfy, soft lullabies playing, everything peaceful. She looked down at Rachael's tiny feet, wiggling out from her blanket, and tilted her head thoughtfully.

Then she said it. "These aren't Barnes feet... I think she has Holter feet."

Dave and I locked eyes, froze for a beat... then bolted into the kitchen like two kids overhearing a juicy secret. Our eyes wide, mouths hanging open, we both whisper-shouted at the same time: "Did you hear that?!?" "Holter feet?!"

I stood there replaying her words in my head. Holter. Not Halter. Not Halder. Holter.

Wait a second... Did Momma Hazel deliberately spell it out as "H-A-L-T-E-R" when she first gave me their names? Had she... hidden the truth? Cloaked it? Buried it? I have been looking for the wrong people all along.

This was the go-to plan I had imagined. Of course, I had thought about hiring a detective—really, I had. I knew they would be expensive, and I would not have the funds for that. I knew I wanted to find them. It was one of my greatest desires. The problem was, I had absolutely no idea—none whatsoever—how to even begin.

In my mind, I'd find Terri's address (I have no idea how), then I would summon up some courage and march right up to her front door... disguised as a saleswoman. Avon, of course. That way, I could knock without suspicion.

She'd open the door, and I'd put on my best "friendly sales pitch" smile. "Good morning! I just wanted to share our new fall colors. Would you like to see the samples?"

And she'd invite me in, because in my imagination, she's gracious like that, and we'd end up at her kitchen table, coffee cups in hand, talking about lipstick shades and nail polish, the way two women do when there's no rush and no reason to hide.

I'd hold up a tiny bottle and say, "How do you like this nail color? I think it would look lovely on you."

In my daydream, I'd fall for her instantly, not in a romantic way, of course, but in the kind of way where your heart recognizes home. Still, I'd restrain myself from leaping across the table and smothering her in a hug. That would blow my cover. There were many other ways of imagining our meeting…

Naturally, in all of my fantasies, we'd quickly become best friends and I'd be invited over to her place the following weekend, and officially become a part of the family, eating potato salad at backyard barbecues.

Okay… so maybe I've got a touch of the daydreamer in me. But if you're going to imagine finding your family, you might as well make it fun.

After finding her, and my siblings, my life would be perfectly complete. All the missing puzzle pieces would finally click into place, and I'd live happily ever after.

Okay… well, maybe I get a little delusional sometimes. But a girl can dream, right?

Our Little Caboose

I must tell you about my Rachael, too. My youngest baby girl was a little firecracker, full of spirit and life—full throttle, all the way. Everything about her ran at 100%. She gave her all to everything she did and to everyone she loved. Her temperament ran the full spectrum—one moment cuddly and happy, the next wildly funny and entertaining, and when she cried, the cries would come as if the world had ended.

God knew I needed a spunky, hilarious, unfiltered yet lovable, caring, kind-hearted little girl who would keep me on my toes every second of every day. Our little caboose made our family complete. A girl filled with wit, warmth, love and laughter.

I remember one afternoon when she was barely three. She decided she was going to "help" me wash the dishes. Within five minutes, she was drenched, covered in suds from head to toe, and insisting on scrubbing everything by herself. By the time we were done, she was more soapy than anything, but she beamed with pride as if we'd just won a medal. That was her—pouring herself into everything, giving her all, and leaving no corner untouched, no heart unloved.

As she grew, she became fiercely competitive, pouring herself into every endeavor and excelling beyond expectation. I remember feeling nervous about having a third child, unsure what it would bring—but God knew exactly how much she would bless our lives.

Miracles can be hidden in sadness

After hearing about the genealogy section at the downtown Dallas library, I decided to make a visit. On January 22, 1991, I hired a babysitter and went. The elevator ride felt like a slow climb toward something mysterious. For so many years, I had carried this longing like a quiet ache, hidden beneath the surface, but ever-present. I was finally doing something about it. I was finally getting close. I spoke with the librarian about my search. She said it's better to do my own recent genealogy research and go back about 2 generations.

Seventy. Years.

I swallowed hard, my voice trembling. "But... I'm adopted."

It was like a door slamming shut, the echo ringing through my bones. My heart sank; my chest tightened. Hope—so carefully carried in with me—crumbled like paper in the rain. The path I thought I'd found vanished into the shadows.

Then, as if sensing my deflation, the librarian added, "But... I do have a few current files from a few states. Let me go check in the back." She was gone for a while, while I nervously paced and waited, looked at my watch, wondered how my kiddos were doing.

She returned quietly; the sound of her footsteps were hushed by the carpet. Her eyes held something I couldn't read—something cautious. Without a word, she handed me a single sheet of paper.

I took it in my hands.

At first, I didn't understand. Then my eyes fell on the title: **DEATH CERTIFICATE.**

It was a record of my mother's death certificate. Emotion overwhelmed me, the finality of the word "death" washed over me like a tidal wave. I was overcome with sorrow, and tears raced down my face. A surge of emotion engulfed me. I had finally found her, but she was already gone. This thing I had chased for so long, this person I had imagined and prayed for and dreamed of, wasn't alive to be found. Joy and sorrow collided so suddenly that I could hardly breathe. My knees went weak. My hands trembled. I couldn't stop the tears. They fell fast, one after another, splashing onto the paper like little echoes of everything I'd lost and longed for.

The search had ended. It shattered me. I had answers, yes. But I also had a sadness so deep it shook the core of my soul.

When I regained my composure, I examined the document. Alameda County was mentioned. But life didn't pause for my heartbreak. I had to pull myself together, leave the library, and get back to the babysitter before baby Rachael woke up hungry. I still needed to pick up the girls, and then Ben from kindergarten, get home, and make them some dinner. The ache in my chest would have to wait—my children needed me.

That night, the kids were all asleep by 8:30, so I made the call to 411 for Alameda County, California. I was able to get a telephone listing for a "C. Holter"

I stared at the number on the scrap of paper in my hand. My fingers trembled. Dave said, "You're so close now. Call the number."

What if I called and they didn't want to know me? What if they saw me as some terrible interruption to their tidy lives? What if I was met with anger... or worse, silence?

Would I be rejected all over again?

I knew my birth mother had wanted to meet me. That truth held me steady. But beyond her—there was only a blur of questions. Would her children—my siblings—want to know I existed? Would I be welcomed or cast aside?

The questions spun through my mind like a storm, each one louder than the last. And still, somehow, I held the number in my hand like a thread of hope. I wasn't sure what I would do next. But I knew my life would never be the same.

I nervously dialed the number.

"Hello?"

"Hello, my name is Camille, and I live in Dallas, Texas. I'm doing some genealogy research; please tell me if you know any of these people…"

The voice on the other end responded, "Yes, I am Chris."

"Well, do you know any of the people I just mentioned?" My heart was pounding as I asked.

Then Chris replied, "Yes, that's my family."

I became choked up as I said, "I'm Camille, your sister."

He replied, "Cool! How ya' been doing?"

We began to talk and to share our lives. We poured out our hearts to each other for almost three hours, as if we could recapture the lost thirty years. "We were told of a sister, Camille, who lived in New Orleans. We thought it was hopeless to find you," Chris shared.

Over the next two months, I had many heartwarming conversations with my newly found siblings. Each call felt like peeling back the pages of a story I was born into but never got to read—until now. My sister Jessica, a journalist, had access to a photo lab at the newspaper where she worked. She arranged to have a copy made of one of the few precious photographs of our mother.

When the envelope finally arrived, my hands trembled as I opened it. Inside was a single black-and-white photograph of her. I just stood there, frozen, staring in awe.

This is her.

The woman I had dreamed about, imagined, longed for... she had a face. A real one. I held the picture up closer, as if getting nearer to the paper might somehow let me step into it. My eyes scanned every detail: the curve of her cheek, the shape of her lips, the light in her eyes. She looked so familiar, yet completely unknown.

I wanted it to be a video, anything that could capture her laugh, her voice, the way she moved. What did she sound like when she was excited or tired or being silly? What kind of stories would she tell me if she were still here? What would she talk about over coffee?

I had answers now... but also so many questions. That single photograph was a treasure, yes, but it was also a doorway into all the things I would never get to know. And yet... I was grateful. For the first time in my life, I could see her.

When Dave arrived home from school that evening, I

showed him the photo of my Mom. He said, "Camille, that looks like you!" I replied, "No, I don't see any resemblance." Dave hollered for Ben to come into the room to see the photo. "Ben," he said, "who is that a picture of?" Ben took one glance at the photo, put his little hands on his hips, looked up, and said, "Dad, you know that's mommy."

I still was not convinced, so that weekend, we got together my camera and some film, and Dave took some photographs of me in the same position. I finished off the role of the film, grabbing some pictures of our little darlings. Next, I had to wait for the film to be developed. This usually took about a week and a half back then. Seemed like forever practically a lifetime when you're young and impatient. When the images came back, I really was surprised.

Miriam (Terri) Theresa Holter   *Camille*

Now, the question imposed in my mind was: did my resemblance to her constantly remind my parents about this lady they wanted to forget about?

One day, Dave looked at me with steady eyes and said, "It's time you met your family face to face. I'll buy you a plane ticket. Take baby Rachael with you, I'll take care of things here with Ben and Bethany."

I could hardly believe it. My heart swelled with gratitude and anticipation. This was it. After a lifetime of wondering and months of unfolding connections, I was going to meet my family.

On March 7, 1991, the long-awaited day finally arrived. As I sat in the car on the way to the Lovefield airport, my hands clasped around the strap of the diaper bag, a quiet kind of electricity buzzed beneath my skin. The highway stretched ahead, but my mind drifted far behind—meandering back over thirty years of questions, prayers, and aching hope.

I thought of all the moments that had led me here, like stepping stones across the waters of time. I thought of the stories I'd been told, the hints and half-truths, and the ache of not knowing.

And then, as if a reel of memory had begun to play, I found myself tracing it all the way back, to The Seven Seas bar, where a kind stranger who called himself "Paul" told a young man named Tommy about his girlfriend...

Chapter 13

Stepping into my Miracle

Before I even understood what the word "adopted" truly meant; I already knew it applied to me. It was part of my identity before I could spell it. Family members said it often, casually: "This is Camille, she's adopted" as if it were just a footnote. But to me, it was everything. I always felt loved, wanted, and even chosen... but I also felt set apart. Different. Marked by that one word.

As I grew older, that difference grew louder.

My adopted family would sometimes talk about their own family heritage. My grandmother was an uptown New

Orleans aristocrat, a real debutant. There was a special ancestry book with a family tree in it.

What started as a quiet curiosity blossomed into something deeper, a relentless ache, a burning need to know. Not just where I came from, but who I came from. Whose eyes I had. Whose laugh might echo in mine. It wasn't just a passing interest; it was a necessary, soul-deep search for belonging.

As the plane soared toward Oakland, California, my emotions swirled like a storm cloud. What would my brothers be like in person? Would they embrace me as family, or would it feel awkward, forced? I longed for my sister to be there too, to complete the picture. In just two months, a lifetime of questions had unraveled into answers. My heart was pounding with excitement, tangled up with nerves I couldn't shake.

As I stepped from the airplane and into the cool, unfamiliar air of California, time seemed to slow. My feet moved forward, but my heart lingered, hovering somewhere between hope and fear. At the bottom of the escalator, I saw them: Forrest and Keith, my older brothers, waiting.

I whispered a quiet prayer into the space between breaths. Please, let them see me. Let them welcome me. Let there be something familiar in my face.

Every step toward them felt like stepping through years of longing, through all the questions I'd carried in silence. And then, there we were: face to face. Strangers tied by blood and story. The meeting was not awkward or tentative as I'd feared; it was instant, magnetic, and filled with warmth. Later that day, we'd gather with Chris, completing a circle that had never truly been broken, only paused.

That weekend, laughter filled the rooms. Real laughter, the kind that rises from shared rhythm, from the knowing without explanation. I spoke, and they understood. I joked, and they laughed with a timing that felt like coming home. I didn't have to explain myself. My humor, once misplaced, fit effortlessly. They were like me. I was like them.

I wanted to bottle it all: the sound of our laughter, the comfort of being seen, the ease of belonging, and keep it forever.

Forrest, Keith, Camille & Chris

But there was something I hadn't expected. In the quiet moments, I'd catch them looking at me. Not just glancing, but studying. Their gazes held something I couldn't quite name. Wonder. Grief. I didn't know how to hold it.

Forrest noticed. His voice came gently, like wind through trees.

"I'm sorry, Camille," he said. "We don't mean to stare. It's just... you're so much like her. Like our mom. The way you speak. The way you laugh. It's like... she's here again."

He paused; his eyes glistened with her memory.

"I wish you could've known her. She was a wonderful person."

That weekend, I began piecing together the story of the woman who gave me life.

I learned that my mother lost her own mother at a young age and was left to shoulder the weight of a home that never felt safe. She became a mother to her brothers and a maid to her father, a hard, unkind man. The walls of her childhood must have felt like a prison, each day a quiet fight for survival. So, when the first window of escape opened, she climbed through it—eloping with a young soldier, desperate for freedom, maybe even for love.

He became the father of Forrest and Keith... and maybe mine too. That part of the story still sits in the shadows. A DNA test could tell us, but we couldn't afford one. Still, the truth doesn't hinge on biology. This man vanished—missing, the military said—and her life moved on, as lives must. Another man entered the picture. Another chapter began.

But as I listened, absorbing these stories of her strength, her sorrow, her survival, I carried a grief that felt impossible to explain. I hadn't known her. Not truly. Not in the way daughters know their mothers. And yet, my heart mourned her as if I had.

I didn't expect anyone to understand the ache I carried that weekend. But then Rosalind, her dear friend, told me something that pierced straight through: my mother had written poems for me. She had mailed packages. She had reached across time and distance with her words and her hands, trying to tell me she loved me, even if I never received a single thing.

She had not forgotten me.

And I never got to tell her: It's okay. I love you. I forgive you. You don't need to carry shame or guilt. I never got to hear her voice, but I knew finally that I was wanted.

That weekend was not just a reunion; it was a reckoning. It was also a learning experience. I found out my Momma was an artist who liked to play the piano and write. I was mourning the mother I would never meet and trying to find peace in the pieces I had been given. And somehow, I did. The truth gave me understanding. The understanding gave me peace.

The past is ever whispering to us. Mine is filled with the stories shared with me.

I had been a tree without any roots, and now I have more roots than I could have ever imagined.

Too soon, it was time to go.

We shared a long, quiet embrace at the airport. Arms wrapped tight around each other, none of us wanting to be the first to let go. It wasn't just a goodbye; it was a binding, a sealing of something long lost, now found.

As I walked toward the gate, I felt something I had never fully known before: wholeness. I had come full circle. And even in the sadness, there was light. I was complete.

My adoptive parents believed it was in our best interest that the woman who gave birth to me have no further rights, no say, no threads left connected. She had signed them away, after all. That was the legal truth, and to them, the emotional one as well.

They weren't acting out of cruelty or selfishness. They were acting out of fear—the fear that one day she might come back and take something from them, take me from them. I understand that now in a way I couldn't back then. The terror of losing a child you've already poured your life into must be unbearable.

I've read those stories, too, modern-day headlines about biological parents resurfacing, custody battles, adoptive families devastated. The fear is real. And in those early years, before open adoptions, DNA kits, and social media, the safest route often seemed to be the most final one: complete severance.

So no, I don't carry bitterness. I don't blame them. How could I? I have no idea what I would have done had the roles been reversed. Adoption isn't clean or simple. The emotions are tangled, layered, stretching far beyond what anyone prepares you for. Love, protection, loss, heartache, gratitude, fear—all of it swirling together over time like sediment in deep water. It doesn't settle easily. Sometimes it never does.

As the plane lifted into the sky, I sat quietly in my seat, the last four days playing across my mind like a film reel on slow spin. So much had changed. I had changed. A part of me that had always felt like a blank page was now filled in, colored, known. I carried that truth gently, like something precious and newly born.

On the plane, next to me sat a kind-faced woman, a stranger at first. She spoke with the casual warmth of someone trying to ease the silence, maybe feeling the weight I carried. And as if by instinct, I began to share my story. Not the polished version, but the real one, raw and recent and unfolding.

We talked for what felt like hours, even though the landing and takeoff in San Diego were brief. It was one of those sacred conversations that needed no preamble or explanation. Just two women, suspended above the clouds, exchanging truth.

Our words were eventually interrupted by the crackle of the intercom, an announcement from the flight attendant. But I knew something in me had shifted. This return flight wasn't just the end of a trip; it was the beginning of a new way of seeing my life, my story, and the people who shaped it.

"As we announced earlier," the flight attendant said over the intercom, her voice chipper but uncertain, "we have a round-trip ticket to give away in appreciation for your re-boarding so quickly in San Diego. We're now back on schedule. Here at Southwest Airlines, we don't usually do this, so I'm not quite sure how to go about it. But if someone would come up here and sing a song, the ticket is yours."

There was a pause, a flicker of surprise among the passengers.

Then, from a front-row seat, a man sprang to his feet and snatched the microphone before anyone else had time to blink. Without hesitation or shame, he bellowed out a crude and off-key version of "Happy Birthday to you…"

All of the passengers fell into a stunned silence. Heads turned. Eyebrows raised. Some passengers exchanged glances that said, surely this doesn't count? It was more spectacle than song.

But rules were rules, and the flight attendant, clearly unsure, handed over the prize with a half-hearted smile. The man strutted back to his seat, ticket in hand.

I turned to the kind woman beside me and whispered, "I wish I'd done that. I would have sung anything. That ticket could've taken me back to see my family again. I don't know when or if we'll be able to afford another trip."

Then I noticed the restroom was finally free and quietly excused myself, still replaying the missed opportunity in my mind.

But wait. When I exited the restroom, something unexpected happened.

The man, the one who had taken the microphone, the one we had all judged too quickly, stood up, turned toward me, and gently handed me the ticket.

"Happy Birthday," he said with a warm smile. The flight attendant got everyone's attention again. "Ladies and gentlemen, it has come to our attention that this young woman has recently found her birth family. And this kind gentleman would like to give her the round-trip ticket he just won.

I was stunned. My hands trembled as I accepted the paper, but it wasn't just a ticket I was holding. It was something more—an unexpected act of kindness from a complete stranger, a full-circle gesture that made my heart swell. I had just left a new family I never knew I had, only to be reminded—midair—that sometimes, people surprise you. Sometimes, generosity sings loud.

Sometimes, miracles find you when you least expect them.

I froze in disbelief. A hush fell over the passengers, quickly replaced by applause. People turned toward me, smiling, clapping, celebrating this unexpected moment of grace. I felt my face flush with awe. The kind woman beside me beamed. It was her. She had shared my story while I was in the restroom. I could hardly believe it.

The cheering crowd began to pass baby Rachael from one set of loving arms to another, each passenger offering smiles, congratulations, and tender words. The cabin had transformed—it wasn't just a plane anymore, it was a celebration in the sky, a floating family reunion, alive with joy and laughter. It felt like a party held midair, where every heart on board was somehow part of the miracle.

The very next week was my birthday. The timing, the ticket, the kindness—it was as if Heaven had reached down and whispered, I've heard your prayers.

When the plane touched down in Dallas, Dave and the children welcomed me home with wide arms and wide smiles. "Mommy's home!" they cheered, clinging to me. My heart was full. I couldn't stop talking—recounting every detail of Oakland, every laugh, every face, every hug. I told anyone who would listen. My soul was lit with something I hadn't felt in years: belonging.

Just days later, a knock came at the door. It was our neighbor, standing on the porch with an envelope in her hand.

"Camille," she said, "I booked this flight to Oakland a while back, but I can't use it—final exams landed right in the middle of it all. I couldn't get a refund, and I thought maybe you could use it."

She paused, smiling. "Oh, and—it's booked for a baby, too."

The old-fashioned paper ticket read Wendy Davis and Baby — May 15, 1991. No one checked IDs back then.

I was stunned. "Of course, I'd love to go," I said, "but Dave will never let me leave again so soon. I just got back. It's too much."

She caught the disappointment in my voice. "Well," she said gently, "just hang on to it. Use it if you can. And if you can't, give it to someone who can." With that, she waved goodbye and disappeared down the walk.

The weeks passed. Three separate times, I nearly gave the ticket away. Each time I thought, I should let this go. It's selfish to keep it. But something—some quiet tug in my spirit—wouldn't let me. I didn't understand it. I only knew I was meant to hold on.

Then came a late-night phone call.

It was my brother Keith. His voice was solemn. Their baby girl, Keri, had been stillborn.

My heart ached. I looked at the plane ticket. The flight was for May 15. The funeral was on May 16.

In my mind, I whispered, "God... you already gave me a round trip ticket for my birthday. Why another? Why this one – on the exact date I needed to go?"

I flew to Oakland once more—this time, not to be reunited with the living, but to mourn the loss of one never known.

At the cemetery, as we stood at Keri's tiny grave, Keith turned to me with tears in his eyes.

"We could never understand," he said softly, "how you could grieve so deeply for someone you never knew. But now... now we get it."

He looked up, toward the sky, and then back at me. "You know," he said, his voice catching, "Keri's in Heaven right now. And Mama—she's rocking her."

He pulled me close and held me in that way only a big brother can.

And for the second time in just two months, grief and grace shared the same space inside my heart.

God has blessed my life in more ways than I could ever fully articulate. His presence has been a steady, guiding hand—

even when I didn't recognize it at the time. In the quiet, uncertain moments, He was already working behind the scenes, preparing hearts, aligning timing, softening paths. He helped me search, and He allowed me to find the answers I had long yearned for—answers that once felt impossibly out of reach. Each step along the journey, He whispered direction into my spirit and led me closer to truth, healing, and a kind of restoration I never dared to hope for.

My big brother Forrest is a quiet man, thoughtful in ways the world rarely notices. A gentle soul with hands that work tirelessly. There's a calm strength in him, a deep thinker with a soft heart. He enjoys chasing sunsets with me and car karaoke. Singing with the Beatles – the BEST! And in those moments, when the light fades and the music fills the air, I'm reminded how lucky I am to have him walking beside me through this life.

Chris is literally the Christopher Robin of our world, wondering around nature capturing amazing photos of flowers and trees. He is one of the finest photographers I have ever known. His images hold a clarity and soul that rival anything you could imagine. When we first met, he was an avid mountain biker, spinning stories that turned every fall into a medal of honor, every misstep into laughter. And I will never forget our first phone call, stretching way past midnight, when it felt as though we had always been family, always belonged to the same story.

Keith is, without a doubt, the Tigger of our circle—bouncing through life with an energy that is impossible to ignore. I fell for his relentless enthusiasm for life, the way he embraces it fully and unapologetically. His smile is ever-present, a beacon of the happiness he carries deep in his soul, touching everyone lucky enough to be nearby. He builds speedways to the sky and is really good at it. But what I love most about him is his profound love for family, the way he treasures each moment.

And Jessica, this girl is a little powerhouse. Sadly, we haven't been able to spend as much time together as I would like, but she will always be my little sister.

During one of our visits, she told me a story. One of those stories you hear it, and feel it in your own bones.

Jessica said:

"We were living in the Bay Area. That morning, my mother woke up unwell and frantic. Her thoughts moved faster than her body, her words spilling out in fragments. During that season, our mom's mental health felt precarious, easily shaken. By then, foster care had already shaped my earliest years. This visit was meant to be a trial, a fragile test to see if I might finally come home.

We had plans to travel to New Orleans that day. My mother told me we were going to find you, Camille. She spoke of you with urgency, with a longing that felt too deep for words, as though finding you, her lost child might repair something time had broken.

We stopped at a busy intersection. Our momma Terri took hold of my wrist and lifted my arm, holding it up as if she were asking a question she no longer knew how to answer. Then she said, simply, to no one in particular, "Who wants this little girl?"

Cars idled. People looked away. A few stared. After several long minutes, a woman stepped out of her car and said she would take me.

I went with her. I remember watching mom disappear back into the crowd, becoming smaller with each step. She didn't turn around. There was no explanation, no promise to return. Only distance.

When I saw our mom again much later, she told me she had gone to New Orleans. I think she took a bus, hoping to catch a glimpse of you, Camille. Just one look. Something to prove that the daughter she had lost was still real.

That was how I was left behind, abandoned without warning, tears streaming down my cheeks.

What stays with me now is not the noise of the street or the faces of strangers. It is the quiet understanding that arrived without words: that a life can be redirected in an instant, that plans dissolve without warning, and that a mother's leaving is not always an act of cruelty. Sometimes it is simply the visible edge of a break that has already happened."

When she told me this, I felt the weight of our age difference settle heavy on my soul. When she was four, I was fourteen... and suddenly, everything made sense. I had been trapped in those strange, suffocating weeks, a lockdown without explanation. Hazel and Tommy had turned into full-time prison wardens, confiscating my freedom, monitoring every movement, acting like I might escape through an air vent. At the time, I thought perhaps they were just Southern parents with a flair for melodrama.

Seventeen years later, Jessica's story snapped the pieces into place with a sickening clarity. My parents weren't being dramatic. They were being hunted.

Terri must have made it to New Orleans.

Back then, almost everything was found in the phone book. White pages for people, yellow pages for businesses. There was NO internet, NO Google, just very public information at your fingertips. Our address and phone number were sitting in the white pages like an open invitation, unless you paid extra for privacy, which my parents hadn't. All she would've needed was a phone book and a little determination.

(Back then, you had to pay extra to be unlisted—something my adoptive parents apparently thought only celebrities or paranoid people did. In hindsight, maybe they should've splurged the few dollars.)

It wasn't melodrama. It was fear. It was two parents trying to protect their child from a woman who was chasing me. This had to be rather unnerving to any parent, especially mine.

Now I can't help but wonder if that had anything to do with our sudden move to Mississippi, (otherwise known, in my teenage mind, as "hillbilly land").

Jessica is a professional writer, a veteran who has served our country, she's been a writer for the Washington Post, is an author and poet, and also a theatrical visionary.

I found not only my missing family but also pieces of myself that had been scattered and lost, along with a legacy and a deeper understanding of where I came from. I feel like God has woven beauty into brokenness and given meaning to questions that had echoed in my soul since childhood.

Although I was never able to meet my birth mother face to face, and I never got to see any of the artwork she created with her own hands, I believe with all my heart that it must have been beautiful—because she was. She raised strong, compassionate, extraordinary children. That alone speaks volumes about the kind of woman she must have been. I grieve the years we didn't have, and I'll always wish I could have told her how much I love her, and how much peace I carry now because of her.

It's my heart's desire to honor her memory, not just with words, but with the work of my own hands. I believe I inherited not only her gifts but also her quiet strength, her creativity, and her sensitivity to the world around her. I want to use those gifts to bless others. I want my art to reach into the hearts of people who are worn down by the chaos of today's fast-paced world and remind them of something beautiful and tender. If I can bring a smile, comfort, or even just a pause for wonder into someone's day, then I know I've carried forward something sacred—something she began.

Chapter 14

Secrets Left on the Curb

For the first time in my life, I felt whole. I had finally found my family. The missing pieces were no longer shadows—faces, names, stories had filled the emptiness. And truth be told, I was at peace not knowing who my birth father was.

Back in the early '90s, when DNA testing first came out, it cost nearly $2,000 for a single test. That wasn't something ordinary people used for patching together their family trees. So, I settled for what I had, and what I had was more than enough: my siblings.

Dave used to say things like, "You ought to go on a talk show, tell your story." Stories of reunions and long-lost families were beginning to surface on television back then, catching the hearts of the curious. But I couldn't bring myself to do it. My parents already carried an obvious disappointment over my search, and the last thing I wanted was to pour salt into a wound that hadn't healed. Some things, I decided, were better left unspoken—at least for a while.

Keith came to visit a few years later. While in New Orleans, my daddy, Tommy, took us on a sentimental tour of the places Keith, Forrest, and Chris had lived as little boys. Later, we went out to lunch at Café Maspero in the French Quarter, where the clatter of plates and chatter of tourists filled the air. My parents weren't angry anymore; maybe time had softened things, or maybe it was simply because my birth mother was gone—and with her, the old threat. Whatever the reason, they welcomed Keith with open arms.

We laughed, swapped stories, and dug into po'boys, dressed the right way, with shrimp piled so high it spilled over the sandwich and across the plate. There's no portion control when it comes to New Orleans eating—just good, messy, southern food at its finest.

I had never told my parents that my birth mother was an artist. It felt like dangerous knowledge, something better left unsaid. Some truths feel too volatile to share, too easily twisted into something sharp. They had been so upset with me already; I didn't want to add more strain to the fragile balance between us. Silence, I decided, was safer.

Maybe that's why it always stung when my requests for art lessons growing up were met with a flat no. I didn't understand why. It wasn't as if I was asking for the moon—just brushes, a canvas, a little guidance. Instead, the doors to art stayed closed.

But other doors opened. They let me join Girl Scouts with my friend Loa, and there, between badges and campouts, I learned to paint in my own rough way. They allowed piano lessons, too, for which I was deeply thankful. The keys became a lifeline—black and white stepping stones across the quiet ache of wanting more.

I babysat, saved, studied, bought supplies when I could, and taught myself. I fed that insatiable appetite for creativity, however possible. And "appetite" is the right word—because I didn't just want art, I hungered for it. I craved it. It was the one thing in me that could not be denied, even when the people I loved most didn't understand it.

Ok, back on track...

Imagine my shock as we stepped out of Maspero's, bellies full of shrimp po'boys, the clatter of plates still buzzing in my ears. We turned toward Jackson Square, the air thick with brass-band echoes and the smell of beignets and coffee. My dad slowed, glanced down the block, and casually said to Keith, "HEY, DID YOU KNOW YOUR MOM WAS AN ARTIST OVER HERE IN THE SQUARE?"

Those words dropped between us like an iron gate slamming shut.

Dave and I were a few steps behind, and I swear it felt like someone had punched me straight in the gut. My heart skipped a beat, my steps faltered. WHAT DID HE JUST SAY? Dave, my steady support, knew how deep this pain ran.

I couldn't believe my ears. I had never told them about her creative side because I didn't want to upset them, or stir up old grief or anger. And here it was, spoken out loud, as if it were nothing.

They knew. They had always known.

And suddenly I realized the silence between us wasn't because they didn't know—it was because they chose not to tell me. Maybe they didn't want to encourage me to be more like her.

When I asked Daddy about the gifts and poetry Rosalind had told me were sent, he didn't flinch. He simply said, "SHE HAD NO RIGHT TO GIVE YOU THOSE THINGS. SHE GAVE UP ALL HER RIGHTS WHEN SHE GAVE YOU AWAY."

"Did she ever see a picture of me?" I asked. "NO."
"Couldn't you have given her one?" Again, just: "NO."

Later, I asked my mom, Hazel, about them. I told her about Rosalind, and how she said Miriam (Terri) had mailed me gifts, letters, and poetry. "WHERE ARE THEY?" I asked.

Her answer was harsh, almost cold: **"I THREW IT ALL AWAY."**

I remember staring at her, stunned. Then said: "Didn't you want to keep them for me? Didn't you even want to open them? DIDN'T YOU THINK THAT MAYBE, ONE DAY, I WOULD WANT THOSE THINGS?

Her only reply was, "NO. IT ALL WENT IN THE TRASH. EVERYTHING."

"Did she get to hold me when I was born?" – **NO**. "Did Terri even get to see me when I was born?" – **NO**.

That was one of the hardest things to forgive—not just that they threw it all away, but the way they did it. The attitude behind it. So harsh, so inconsiderate of what I might want. Here was a woman who gave them her child, her daughter became their daughter, and they couldn't even save the gifts she sent.

Gifts from a mother to her child.

I still can't wrap my mind around it. My parents were loving and caring people, despite their flaws and struggles. But this—this felt like hate. Or if not hate, then some other word I don't even have.

And yet, even in that devastation, I had to find a way forward. Forgiveness did not come easily, it was not one prayer, one tear, and done. It was years of returning to that memory, years of wrestling with the bitterness that tried to take root.

In some strange way, their harshness drove me deeper into creativity. The more they resisted, the more I clung to it. And it shaped me—into an artist who creates not only out of joy, but out of survival.

Trust... that was harder. I learned not to expect tenderness where shame or silence stood guard. But I also learned that sometimes love and brokenness can live in the same house, under the same roof, in the same two people. My parents did love me. They raised me, fed me, clothed me, and laughed with me. But they were also afraid—maybe even threatened—by the woman who gave me life.

And so, the gifts went in the trash. But the gift that truly mattered, the unexplainable, uncontainable need to create, stayed with me. It had already been planted too deeply (into my DNA) that it couldn't be thrown away.

Chapter 15

The End of the Road

At the very end of his life, my daddy Tommy paid for a DNA test. There was someone in my life who was insisting that he was my biological father, and I had no way to prove this person wrong. I was tired of this argument; it lasted nearly 20 years. Daddy had always told me he was NOT my biological father, and I believed him. I never thought he had a reason to lie. The results came back: 99.9% certainty that Tommy was **not** my biological father.

Tommy and I were never as close as I wished we could have been. But toward the end, we both tried to mend things.

Sometimes he'd come over on weekends when we grilled out, or if we had a big sack of crawfish to eat. We'd sit together, messy hands, messy hearts, trying to patch up years that had left us distant.

By then, cancer had hollowed him out, and doctors filled his days with pain meds.

My Aunt Karen (his sister) came by while I was there. He wanted to get the trailer "fixed up" before he died. So, I went to stay with him for a few days to help. Even as the cancer drained his strength, he refused to be idle. He carried around a to-do list of things he wanted finished. He'd say, Camille, please paint this room." Karen, "Would you wash and iron all the drapes? He was still trying to mend the world in small ways before leaving it behind.

One day, the three of us made a trip to the home supply store to pick up a few things. The drive was quiet, sunlight falling across his hands on the steering wheel. The disease had aged him terribly; at sixty-one, he looked closer to one hundred.

When we finished shopping, my aunt and I waited with the cart as he pulled the truck to the loading area. He insisted on loading everything himself, long strips of shoe molding, paint supplies, odds and ends. None of it was heavy, but still, strangers passing by gave us sharp looks, and evil eyes as if to say, why aren't you helping that poor old man?

They didn't know what I knew, that this was his way of holding on, of being strong for as long as he could. I watched him load those boards, my heart sinking. Here was a man who was slipping from this world, using the last of his strength to make sure my momma would have something left behind: a trailer fixed up enough to rent, a little income to carry her through.

Growing up, money was something we never talked about. Five kids, one income, and a mother who sewed our clothes, collected hand-me-downs from cousins, and stretched every penny. I sometimes think that woman may have invented copper wire, she could stretch a penny so tight it squeaked. I remember being in junior high with only two pairs of pants. One pair, yellow bell-bottoms, was stained and worn. I used to wish for new hand-me-downs but didn't dare ask. One day, Mama opened my closet and said softly, "My, you sure don't have very many clothes." That was the first time she noticed.

Now, watching Daddy work himself to exhaustion, I understood the quiet desperation beneath those years. He wanted to leave her with something solid: a trailer to rent, a home to live in, and maybe a bit of peace to ease his conscience. His last week, I stayed with him. He cycled between good days and bad ones. On the good days, he'd eat a little or let me make him smoothies. On the bad days, he refused everything.

One afternoon, I offered again, "Daddy, let me make you a smoothie."

"No," he said.

"Then let me take you to the hospital. They can at least give you IV fluids."

Again, he shook his head. Then he asked quietly, "Do you think God speaks to you?"

"Yes," I said. "Why? What did God say to you, Dad?"

He told me, "To hurry up."

I didn't know how to argue with that.

My daddy Tommy had done many bad things in his life, but despite it all, there was a part of him that was good. He never bragged, never spoke ill of others. His heart, for all its storms, carried a gentleness that showed itself in quiet ways. If a family was hungry, he fed them. If someone needed a hand, he offered it. He was rough around the edges, but there was still something in him trying to build good out of subversion.

One evening, after his friends had left, he and I sat together in the quiet. He told me he was sorry for all the pain, for the years lost between us. He asked me to forgive him. I cried and told him I already had. Then I asked if I could speak at his funeral.

He replied, "Well, what do you want to say?"

I told him about the card I once made for him, covered in butterflies, with a tiny caterpillar drawn along the bottom edge, and a scripture wrapping around it: "If any man be in Christ, he is a new creation. Old things are passed away; behold, all things are become new." I told him I wanted people to hear that story, to see how that card represented his life, that God had changed him, and that now he was ready to go home.

He smiled faintly. "Okay," he said. "You can say that."

Friday came and he scratched the last thing off of his "to do" list. We then drove him out to McNeil. He wanted to die in the family country home, where the quiet fields could cradle him. He told us God would take him home on Sunday. Family gathered—sisters, brothers, nieces, and nephews. My son brought his guitar and strummed soft hymns for his Pepaw. We didn't know what to say or how to handle the heavy silence. It didn't seem fair. I had just begun to have a father, just one year of closeness, and now he was slipping away. But cancer doesn't discriminate. And sure enough, on Sunday, just as dad had said, God took him home.

That Sunday night, the coroner came for his body. The next morning, I loaded the kids into the van and started the long drive home. No one said much. The car felt heavy with silence, the kind that presses against your chest and won't let go.

Later that week, I had to pick my kids up early from school so we could drive to Mississippi for the wake. After arriving at the school, I opened the van door and froze.

There, on the ground, lay a butterfly. Perfect, still, as if it had been waiting for me.

I bent down, half afraid it would crumble at my touch, but it didn't. Its wings quivered lightly, alive. I lifted it gently and placed it on the dashboard.

When the kids climbed in, they gasped. "Where did that butterfly come from?" they asked. "How did it get here?"

I told them the truth, I didn't know. It had let me pick it up and set it there, and somehow, it felt like a sign.

The butterfly rode with us the whole way to Mississippi, wings trembling softly each time the van hit a bump. I kept glancing at it, half expecting it to fly off, but it stayed.

After the wake, I leaned over to my son, Ben; "Go see if the butterfly's still on the dashboard," I whispered. "If it is, bring it inside."

He came back a few minutes later, hands cupped around the delicate creature. "What should I do with it?" he asked. I told him, "Put it on Pepaw's chest." Ben walked up to the casket and placed it gently on my daddy's button-up shirt. It rested there, wings slowly opening and closing, next to the folded newspaper with the crossword puzzle he had left unfinished, and the ballpoint pen tucked neatly in his pocket.

The next morning, when we walked back into the funeral home, people were whispering, asking where the butterfly had come from. It stayed there the entire ceremony, still as if it understood. When I stood to speak, I told them about the card, about the scripture, about the butterfly on my dashboard. It was a small miracle, but a powerful one, it felt like heaven had reached down to touch the earth.

A few days later, Tina, Becky, and I decided to spend some time together before Becky had to fly back home. We arrived at Tina's house, and the kids buckled up in the van, buzzing with excitement for a day out. Tina handed baby Kayla to Becky and said, "Will you pop the back van window open so I can load up the stroller?"

"Sure, Tina," I replied.

She ran inside to grab the stroller and diaper bag. Then it happened: a butterfly fluttered into the van and landed on the dashboard. Everything fell quiet. I glanced at the backseat; all the kids were staring in disbelief at this delicate creature. Becky looked at me, her eyes mirroring the same awe I felt.

The butterfly lingered on the dashboard for a moment longer, then lifted off and disappeared, leaving us all a little breathless in its wake.

About a week later, I opened the small box of things my Daddy left me. Simple things he wanted me to have, a small piece carved from ebony, a few books, some depression glass, and a cloisonné dish decorated with flowers and three butterflies. That's when I really needed the Kleenex!

I don't know why God sent the butterflies, but I do know they carried peace into our grief. They were whispers from heaven, gentle, unmistakable reminders that Daddy was safe, whole, and finally free.

Not long after, I went to see Tina. She was heartbroken with grief, tears spilling as she said, "I don't know what to do. This grief is so bad, I don't know how to handle it."

I gave her the only answer I could think of, "Find a closet. Go in. Just you and God. Cry, talk, tell Him everything. Tell Him how much it hurts."

A week later, I went back to check on her. When she opened the door, her face was glowing. She smiled and exclaimed, "I found a closet! —and it worked. It really worked!"

Matthew 6:6 KJV

But thou, when thou prayest, enter into thy closet, and when thou hast shut thy door, pray to thy Father which is in secret; and thy Father which seeth in the secret shall reward thee openly.

When you hear from God for yourself, everything changes.

Chapter 16

The Road with No Signs

After my dad passed, I had time to reflect back on how things were for us as young children. Our father was a provider in the old sense: money came, necessities appeared. He wasn't often emotionally there for us, but we understood that he was a busy man with different priorities. Grief excavates what we have buried without knowing, that hole in the heart where only he could fit, where no one else will ever belong. He was the only dad I ever had, and I guess that's why. I continued with the dull ache of realizing there would never be another chance, but also peace in knowing that he had made it to heaven.

Camille, Becky and Tina

The five of us traveled the roads of childhood together: Becky, Tina, Tommy, Timmy, and me. We were meandering wayfarers, stumbling along through life without a map, trying to follow roads no one had paved before us. Reminding me of those old dirt roads when we lived on, out "in the sticks". Dusk descended with no landmarks to anchor us, no mile markers to measure our progress, no sense of arrival or direction. Even when you think you might be going the right direction, there's no confirmation. You just keep moving, trusting that somewhere ahead, the fog will lift.

There were hazards, too. You might drive through a flood zone without knowing it. There are no warnings about sharp curves or washed-out bridges. And then there were the emotional pitfalls, the ones that live in the body rather than the landscape. They creep up inside you. The anxiety of not knowing where you are, the fear that grips you when you realize no one else does either. The constant guessing. You learn to rely on instinct, but instinct alone doesn't promise you'll find your way. Somewhere between panic and persistence, you discover that survival is less about direction and more about endurance.

Growing up as the eldest of five, I became "the helper." A title that sounds quaint until you realize it's an unpaid internship in household management with no possibility of promotion. My little hands that stirred the pot, folded the laundry, wiped the counters. I wiped faces still soft with baby fat. I was the one who made sure my younger siblings had their hair brushed, their baths drawn, and toys put away. I carried this responsibility because our Momma struggled with depression for many years. Some days she moved through the house like a shadow, distant, quiet, unreachable. It fell to me to keep things running. Responsibility was handed to me too soon and too early. I wore it like a badge, never realizing how heavy it was.

When I look back now, I see just how little I knew. I didn't know how to be a good sister. I don't remember board games or lying in the grass, making up stories about clouds and giving them names. My life was filled with duty, not delight. We were children walking a road with no signs, no one to whisper which turn might lead to love or laughter.

The road stretched before us like a gray ribbon disappearing into fog. Some days it felt endless. You strain your eyes to see just a few feet ahead, thinking maybe this time the path will become clear, but it never really does. You keep moving, not because you know where you're headed, but because stopping feels worse. We were wanderers without a compass, learning to survive by feelings, not by light.

The four-year gap between me and my next sibling, Becky, felt vast, an expanse where I stood alone, neither fully child nor quite capable, suspended in that strange place between dependence and duty.

Let me tell you about little Becky. She was the spark plug of the family, with more energy in her little finger than the rest of us had combined. Becky had her share of mischief as a youngster. She and Tina would fight like wildcats, pinching, mocking voices, calling names, making faces and the teasing could spark a fight just as easily as a slap. But Becky had a way of melting your heart right after she made you want to pull your hair out; she'd go from hollering to hugging in seconds flat. Mischief and kindness lived side by side in her.

Timmy, on the other hand, was gentle to his core. When we were little, he followed me like a shadow, trusting I knew the way. I wish I'd realized he wasn't just tagging along; he was reaching out. I was too busy keeping everything running to see that what he needed most was for me to stop and simply be with him. As the boys grew older, Timmy and Tommy were as inseparable as Siamese twins, always side by side. Tommy, his big brother, he adored.

Life wasn't kind to Timmy. Our father, Tommy, was especially hard on him, though I never knew why. Watching

Timmy take it quietly, without lashing back, made me both admire him and ache for him. I'll never forget the morning we couldn't find him anywhere, until we discovered him curled up in the doghouse, asleep among a litter of puppies. That was Timmy: finding comfort in the quietest corners, turning chaos into peace.

We were doing the best we could with the limited instruction manual we'd been given, tripping over each other while pretending we weren't lost.

And then, years later, after I became a mother myself, that road with no signs stretched out all over again. My son Ben was the first to hold a mirror to that part of me. He came home one afternoon, cheeks red from playing at the park with his friend Willie and Willie's mom, Wendy. His voice was light with truth when he said, "Momma, Ms. Wendy is a play mom. You are just a work mom."

Those words rang like a bell through my soul, they resonated to the deepest part of my soul. I wasn't sure how to change a lifetime of habits but I didn't want to be a mom who failed my children.

You move forward with the best instincts you have, praying the turns you make will lead your children toward safety, joy, and home. I read parenting books, took parenting classes, and did the best I could to learn what to do, and how to do it.

Dave carried the fun side of life that I never quite learned. He was the one who made up funny nonsense words that sent the kids into fits of laughter. Out of nowhere he might belt out a course of the song "Shaving Cream". Every morning became a race to the kitchen, the first one awake enough to yell, "Ducka, ducka, yont to? One to five, beat you to it!" was the winner—though what they actually won, no one ever knew. Dave had a way of turning the ordinary into a game, a celebration.

Where I leaned toward structure and lists, he brought the silliness and laughter. Beyond the fun, he also spoke truth into their lives, with a steady wisdom that pointed them forward. In all the places I felt I fell short; he filled the gaps.

As we grew older, my dad had left church and was traveling the path that leads to destruction again. His drinking had worsened, a slow-motion collision we all witnessed but no one possessed the tools to stop. Daddy became a dangerous detour my siblings kept taking, following him down side roads that led nowhere good. I was never extended these particular invitations, never asked to join the wreckage. I stayed on the shoulder while they sped past. I told myself, in those moments of watching from the sidelines, that if love required destruction as its price of admission, I'd rather stay uninvited. So, they followed him down treacherous paths, participated in things they knew carried consequences, all for the chance at connection, that fleeting sense of approval.

They'd follow any road he walked, no matter how dark, no matter where it led. It nearly destroyed them, those roads. Took them places they spent years trying to return from.

And sometimes, in my darker moments, I wondered if the love they sought was worth the wreckage it required. I also understood why they couldn't stop themselves from trying. When you're lost and someone offers to lead, you don't ask where they're going. You just follow, hoping they know the way.

Tina and Tommy's lives had been disturbingly chaotic from the start. By the time they were grown, the damage was already done, stitched into their souls by people who never meant to hurt them, but did anyway. My younger siblings had it bad, especially after I moved away. Each of them carried their own battles, their own scars. There were years when it felt like everyone was fighting their own demons while simultaneously trying to battle everyone else's. The weight of it all could have broken them, but somehow, they rose above it. Both Tommy and Tina died at an early age and I miss them more than anything. I grieve that they are gone, but also that they lost the chance to have a wonderful life.

Becky was able to find strength in in her heart wherein others would have given up. She turned her pain into purpose and built a life filled with grace and quiet resilience. She's faithful, a fabulous mother and Nana, pouring herself into her family with everything within. Her love runs deep and steady, she shows up for her loved ones in the big moments and the small ones as well, the way only someone who's experienced both loss and grace can. My baby sister, Becky now embraces every blessing that comes her way with joy and gratitude.

Timmy, likewise refused to let the darkness define him. He has built something remarkable out of the ashes—a thriving business along the Gulf Coast, leading a crew of men who restore boats. What began with nothing but grit and the broken parts of his life became a story of determination and redemption. Where others might have rained on his parade, he saw possibility. Watching him steer his own course, steady and sure, makes a big sister deeply proud of the man he's become.

Looking at Becky and Timmy now, I can't help but feel proud: proud of how far they've come, proud of their courage, proud of the light they carry after walking through so much darkness, and proud that they didn't let it destroy them.

Chapter 17

New Highway Under Construction

Over the next thirty years, my relationship with my biological family grew in ways I could never have imaged. My relationship with Momma Hazel grew stronger too. As time went on, I began to see my parents differently. I realized they'd been doing the best they could with the hand life dealt them, a hard hand, marked by loss and disappointment. Somewhere along the way, my anger softened into compassion.

No one really understands why life has to be so hard sometimes; it just is. We live in a world where good and bad blur together, where people carry both kindness and brokenness in the same heart. My parents eventually accepted that I had two families, and that I loved them both.

Sometimes we'd pack up the van and drive all the way to California; other times, they'd come down to Texas or Louisiana. Slowly, new connections began to stitch themselves into the old fabric of my life. One of my favorite moments was when Momma Hazel finally got to meet all of my brothers at a special event we held. To see her surrounded by them, faces she'd only heard about in fragments, felt like watching two worlds collide and finally embrace.

Meanwhile, Dave and I were raising our three children. The highways and byways of life had their bumps and detours, but somehow, we kept moving forward.

Keith, Forrest, Hazel, Camille, and Chris

In the middle of it all, Forrest and Keith learned a truth that hit like a lightning bolt: their father hadn't died after all. He'd abandoned them, moved back to Minnesota, remarried, and vanished from their lives. To this day, none of us even know if he ever divorced our mother. The discovery was sharp, painful, and yet another reminder that families are complicated maps, some roads paved, some broken, some washed out and some just ending without warning.

I never expected another chapter to my story—not at this stage of life. And yet… the page turned.

In 2019, it was my youngest daughter, Rachael, who set the

next chapter in motion. Always curious and always looking a little deeper, she had an intense desire to understand her family's health history. She decided to take the 23andMe DNA test. I thought nothing of it at the time, just another one of Rae's projects. She received the results and made it public on the 23andMe public platform.

A surprise yes, but the surprise wasn't in the health results. It came in the form of a message from a stranger named Brandon.

"We're closely related," he wrote. "But I have no idea who you are."

Rachael was just as baffled. I don't know either... my mom was adopted. Maybe it's a connection there, or on my dad's side of the family.

Mom: I saw "Sweet Baby Rae" pop up on my phone screen. Normally, our conversations are light and casual, but this call was different. Rae's voice was chipper, like she had aced another exam or was about to tell me she'd found a new cookie recipe.

No thunderclap. No trembling soundtrack. Just her steady,

cheerful voice dropping the words into my lap like a boulder: "I'm pretty sure I found your father's family." Who would have ever thought she would call to tell me she'd uncovered an entire one-half branch of my bloodline?

At first, I thought I misheard. My mind scrambled to keep up as Rae spilled out details, weaving names and connections, sketching fragments of lives that suddenly might belong to me. She explained Brandon's message and her new role as DNA detective.

But inside, I froze. The air grew thin, the room too small. It felt like the floor had shifted beneath me, and I hadn't yet found my balance. I was stuck between disbelief and panic. I wasn't ready. I hadn't braced for this.

Rachael insisted I take the test too—maybe it would connect the dots. Perhaps it would explain the unexplainable. Maybe it would fill in some missing pieces, perhaps it would rule out a few wild theories. But waiting was agony, the kind of restless anticipation where you're standing at the edge of something mysterious, unable to see what's on the other side.

While we waited, Rachael and Brandon continued their DNA

research. Our "DNA detectives" dove headfirst into research like two rookie detectives straight out of an NCIS Episode. They scoured family trees, digging through charts, cross-referencing names, and chasing whispers of the past. They called each other late into the night like they were chasing down a fugitive instead of some family history. I halfway expected them to buy trench coats, fedoras, and magnifying glasses on Amazon. Brandon would call Rae with updates like he was cracking a cold case, and Rachael was right there with him, studying the science of it all, and throwing around words like "centimorgans" as if we were all supposed to know what that meant.

Through the rumor mill, word started spreading about this new "mystery relative" popping up on 23andMe.

DNA is pretty amazing when you think about it. It's like this tiny code tucked inside every cell that not only makes you who you are but can also tell an incredible story about your past. With just a simple test, DNA can reveal where your ancestors lived, connect you to relatives you never knew you had, and even point out little quirks or health traits you've inherited. What's wild is that all of this—your looks, your health tendencies, your family connections—is wrapped up in the same strands that make every human unique, yet still tie us all together. It's like a personal roadmap and a family album all rolled into one.

 Maybe it would reveal some of the scientific quality needed to help with the investigation. Qualitative analysis. While we waited for my results, Brandon thought perhaps one of his aunts could be my mother.

But Rae quickly corrected him: "No, Mom already knows who her birth mother was. Terri stayed in touch with her adoptive family. She's met her siblings. That story is already written."

It turns out that DNA testing isn't just a swab of the cheek, it's an exit ramp you didn't see coming, straight into a new stretch of highway you weren't prepared to travel. Then my results came in. And with them, a name I had never seen before.

The test determined that a woman named Carolyn was my half-sister. That's where things got strange. I was born in 1961, but her father had died in 1958. That math didn't add up, no matter how many times I turned it over in my head. The only logical "DNA conclusion"? We must share a mother... but that didn't fit, because I knew—without a shadow of a doubt—that Miriam Theresa "Terri" Jane Brenner Holter was my biological mother.

How could she be Carolyn's, too?

It was as if the ground tilted beneath me, changing everything I thought I knew. A million thoughts collided at once—shock, confusion, questions that locked themselves tight. That door was locked tight in my mind, a door I never touched, never leaned against, never opened, keys nowhere in sight. Every answer slipped from my grasp like Jell-O through chopsticks: ridiculous, and impossible to hold.

I had never imagined this moment before. Not yet. Not ever. The story I had carried about myself—solid, certain, suddenly felt flimsy, like a photograph bleached by too much sun.

Was Terri not who I thought she was? Or was there another truth—messier, more hidden—lurking in the shadows of our family's past?

That left only one possibility: someone in Brandon's family was my biological father. But who? And so, the sleuthing began in earnest. Brandon pestered relatives, checked with cousins, uncles, anyone who might have a faint memory of a young woman named Terri being in New Orleans around 1960. The family history he uncovered was full of jagged edges: suicide, too many children raised by one exhausted mother, and siblings who had scattered in all directions. It felt like chasing ghosts, but Brandon wasn't ready to quit.

And then—breakthrough. As it turns out half-sisters share 25% DNA, but so does an aunt. They discovered that Carolyn was actually my aunt and not my half-sister. This means that one of her brothers was in fact my biological father.

I wanted to be grateful. I tried to match Rachael's excitement, to thank her for the hours she poured into searching, the love she showed in finding what we once thought unfindable. But what rose in me wasn't gratitude. It was a twisting, heavy anxiety that pressed against my ribs and whispered, this is too much, too soon, revealing things I wasn't ready for.

Sometimes, when the questions became unbearable, I would just imagine what it would be like to sit across from my birth mom. If only I had a time machine, I'd go back to when Miriam (Terri) was still alive. I'd find her. I'd sit in some coffee shop, lean across the table, and listen to her stories—the real stories—the ones she had kept locked away.

In my mind, it always unfolded the same way:

The bell above the café door gave a weary chime as I stepped inside. The air was thick with coffee and something buttery, like pie fresh from the oven. I scanned the room, searching strangers' faces for the one I'd never seen in person but carried in my bones.

And then—I saw her.

Miriam.

She sat in a corner booth, posture graceful but unguarded, one hand wrapped around a steaming mug. Morning light spilled across her face, catching strands of hair. My heart slammed against my ribs.

For a moment, I froze, afraid she'd vanish if I blinked. I memorized every detail; the soft tap of her fingers on the cup, the faraway look in her eyes—as if she were both here and not here.

I walked toward her, each step fragile, like the air might break.

"Mind if I sit?" I asked softly.

She looked up, her eyes studying me in a way that made me feel both seen and sifted through. Her lips curved into the faintest smile. "Please."

I slid into the seat across from her. The café faded. My breath was loud in my ears.

"I've come a long way to meet you," I whispered.

Her expression shifted, unreadable. "And why is that?"

Emotion tangled in my voice as I said, "Because you're my mother. I guess I heard your heart beating from the beginning, and I know that I've always felt it."

The words hung between us, fragile as glass.

She lowered her gaze, fingers tightening around the mug.

"I've wondered," she said quietly, "if one day you'd find me. I've thought about what I would say."

"Then say it now."

Her eyes lifted, filled with something deep, unnameable. In that moment, I knew there were whole chapters of her life locked away in shadows.

And then—she was gone.

The café dissolved. The clink of silverware, the scent of coffee, the sunlight—all vanished.

Okay... so maybe I'm a dreamer. But if you're going to imagine finding your family, you might as well make it interesting.

Chapter 18

Proceed with Caution

The searches continued for Rachael and Brandon. And the woman, Aunt Carolyn, reached out to her nephews, Cameron and Devlin, who had already done 23andMe but kept their profiles private. When she told them about me, they went online to make their profile public, which immediately showed that my DNA matched theirs. It was the official, drumroll please: game-changer. At that point, it confirmed them as my brothers, and Dennis Carlson was my father. Just like that, in the blink of an eye, a lifetime mystery was completely solved. The unexplainable was explained, the marvel of science, and the fascinating DNA structure that's built into each of us.

Another late arrival to my story. Another door that opened too late for me to walk through.

Just like with Terri, he was already gone.

I came too late.

Again.

Now that I have learned about Dennis, I felt sad that he had already passed away. It wasn't the same devastation as losing my Momma Terri, because I'd never lived with the anticipation of finding my dad. Still, there was a pang, a sharp ache. I would never know what it was like to have a father, not really. It would've been something, maybe even wonderful to have known him. But this time, at least, I wasn't left empty-handed. This time, I have five new siblings.

I am the oldest of five in my adopted family, the middle of five on my mother's side, and, wouldn't you know it, the oldest of six (that I know of) on my father's side.

Dennis left behind a trail of siblings for me, aunts, and stories waiting to be uncovered. My Aunt Sue and Aunt Becky were among the first to reach out. They came down to New Orleans for a little vacation, and we met for lunch. Short visit, yes—but rich. I liked them right away. Over salads and stories, I got my first taste of who Dennis was: complicated, restless, brilliant in some ways, but always wrestling with his own storms.

Walking in Darkness and Fog

After Hearing About Dennis

I didn't see it coming. First came the SHOCK! Then the shock moved to grief, for years gone, for all of the conversations that would never happen. Guilt, for not feeling the joy Rachael surely hoped I would feel. Frustration—for learning about a father I would never meet, a life we would never share. And sadness—sharp and undeniable—for the lost opportunities that could never be claimed.

Each step was uncertain, the path ahead obscured. The world was muted, shadows pressing in from all sides, and I couldn't see where I was going or how I would get there. Every familiar landmark of my life, the memories, the certainties, the version of myself I thought I knew —was blurred, almost unrecognizable.

I had felt this sadness before, when my birth mother's death certificate was handed to me. At first, I thought my grief came from years of waiting, a lifetime of hope, from the long-held anticipation of meeting her. I had heard about her all my life. I knew she loved me, and wanted to know me. And now, that would never happen. When a lifetime of hopes is suddenly dashed, grief is inevitable.

But this time, it hit me broadsided, like a freight train, reminding me that some losses don't come with warning. I moved forward slowly, one tentative step at a time, feeling lost yet drawn onward, as if the fog itself held pieces of a story I had yet to uncover. Some moments were sharp and piercing, like stumbling over roots I hadn't seen, while others were quiet and hollow, like stepping into a space that should feel familiar but didn't.

For days afterward, I carried it in silence. I replayed Rachael's words in my mind, her voice echoing as if it had rearranged the air around me. My life suddenly felt more complicated—a story with a whole missing chapter I hadn't asked to read. It was like being handed a family portrait with my face sketched into the corner, recognizable, but drawn in lines I didn't yet know. A family that was mine, and yet not mine.

I began to understand why some people pull back when they find their biological relatives. These people don't always "feel" like family at first—they are strangers who happen to share your DNA. Science can draw lines on a chart, but it can't build a bond. Bonds are built in time spent together—the jokes, the hugs, the fights, the forgiveness. Those are the pieces that fit together to make a real family.

I told myself timing mattered, and it did. Curiosity alone isn't readiness. Readiness is about emotional safety—about choosing the pace of your own healing. Being handed a truth before you're ready is like being thrown into floodwaters before you've learned to swim. You flail, you gasp, you wonder if you'll make it to shore.

For weeks, I sat with the news in silence, numb and disoriented. At times, I felt given away all over again, forgotten, like I'd landed in a world I did not belong to. And yet even in my resistance, I knew this: once a door has been opened, you can't pretend it isn't there. You can't unknow what you've learned. My new family was real. I had brothers and sisters—living, breathing people—and I owed it to myself to try to know them.

My story took a hairpin turn I never saw coming.

The days that followed were quieter. I carried the truth like a stone in my pocket, aware of its weight with every step. Everyone had always assumed my father could've been Robert Holter or Chris's dad. I asked Forrest and Keith what they could recall from their childhood—any clues, any scraps of memory about who my father might have been. No one knew for sure. With Keith only sixteen months older than me, and Chris just fifteen months younger, it seemed likely that I shared a father with one of them. But the days of "free love" were abundant back then.

For the next three decades, I never gave it much thought. What once seemed impossible was suddenly undeniable.

Looking back, I was dumbfounded. There were more questions than answers, more puzzle pieces than places to fit them. No stories from the past had prepared me for this kind of revelation—a truth was now extremely complicated.

On my dad's side, the very first sibling I met after all those years was a sister.

And here's where the universe decided to show off its sense of humor.

Her name?

Brace yourself.

Camille.

Yes, you read that right. Out of all the names in the world, my sister and I share the exact same one. I've only met maybe three other Camilles in my whole sixty years (okay,

okay—forty-nine, if you go by my official timeline). But here she was: another Camille, my flesh and blood. How could that even happen? Coincidence, or some cosmic wink from above?

This Camille shared my blood.

The name I had carried my entire life — stitched into report cards, whispered across playgrounds, signed at the bottom of love letters and legal documents — suddenly wasn't mine alone. It was hers too. It had always been hers too.

And somehow, without knowing it, we had been answering to the same sound all along.

When she asked how she'd find me at the airport, I told her, "Don't worry. I'll be in a white Murano. You'll figure it out." But when I pulled up to the arrivals curb, I decided to have a little fun. I leaned against the car, holding a homemade sign that read:

"Hey—I'm Camille, and I'm looking for Camille."

I can't tell you how long I stood there, but every minute was pure entertainment. Strangers walked past, craning their necks, trying to make sense of it. Some laughed, some looked downright confused, and more than a few gave me that side-eye glance you reserve for people who might be just a little unhinged. Not one person asked what it meant, which made it even funnier.

And then, I saw her. My sister Camille walked out, spotted the sign, and her face froze for half a second before breaking into the widest grin. The hug we shared erased years of not knowing each other. It was one of those bone-deep hugs that makes time collapse, as if you're trying to gather up every lost year and squeeze it into one embrace.

My new sis is the kind of person you can't help but find interesting—she loves to fly like our dad did, slices across the water on skis, and somehow manages to keep biking even after an injury that would've sidelined most people. She's bubbly and outgoing, yet carries this calmness too, like she could chat your ear off one minute and then quietly solve all of life's problems the next. Honestly, she makes the rest of us look like underachievers.

Why do my sister and I share the same name? The only explanation I can imagine is this: Terri must have stayed in touch with Dennis, and at some point, she told him about the baby girl Tommy and Hazel had adopted. I can almost hear her voice in a letter or a phone call, letting him know, "They finally have their baby. After all the heartbreak, after all the miscarriages, this one is theirs."

Terri ostensibly had kept in touch with Tommy and Hazel. They had even babysat Forrest and Keith while I was in the hospital. They were good people, steady and kind, and they were overjoyed to finally hold a child of their own. After so many losses, this baby must have felt like a miracle. They named her Camille.

And so, in that tangle of lives and coincidences, my sister and I carried the same name—two Camilles, connected by mystery, by family, by choices made in shadows that still ripple through my memory. My new sister's features echoed my daughter's. My laugh resembles hers. Suddenly, another family story was layered over the one I already knew. Each connection was a puzzle piece, waiting to find its place.

Soon after, Aunt Carolyn flew into New Orleans to meet us too. She booked a hotel nearby—declared it too forward to stay with us since, technically, I was still a stranger—but that didn't stop her from jumping straight into family mode. We did touristy things, visited one of my favorite plantation homes (though we missed the gardens because the sun set too quickly), and shared a phenomenal dinner with Aunt Carolyn, Camille, Dave, and our kids. Rachael couldn't be there, school had her crazy busy, that was bittersweet, because she was the one who had cracked this whole case open.

After meeting Camille, I started noticing the small ways family shows itself, some in thoughtful, quiet brilliance, some in warmth and exuberance. Ian, for example, is a sweet soul. (He's Camille's son, my new nephew.) One of the first times I got to meet him, he was so excited that he was dancing, skipping, and jumping for joy all around the house. I don't think anyone could have received a more wholehearted, exuberant welcome. His happiness was contagious, lighting up the room and reminding me that family isn't just about history or shared blood, it's about these moments of pure, unfiltered connection, laughter. My new sibling relationships are layered with curiosity, history, and sometimes awkwardness. Ian embodies immediate, unguarded love and happiness.

Not long after, Dave announced it was time for a road trip to Minnesota to meet more of the family. We turned it into a mini-vacation: stopped in Memphis to see a friend, lingered a day in St. Louis (by the way, the Gateway Arch, it is massive in person, way more imposing than in photos). From there, it was on to Aunt Sue's, in Elk River, Minnesota.

Driving through the cornfields of Iowa feels like entering a dream that's been looping since the dawn of time. The road stretches so straight it almost dares you to find a curve, and the corn on either side rises up, rows and rows upon rows golden corn catching the light. After a while, you start to imagine they're whispering about you as you pass, the way small-town folks do when something unfamiliar rolls through.

The air smells like dirt and sun, like something honest and unpretentious. For a while, it feels like the world has been boiled down to its essentials: land, sky, motion, and thought.

But after a few hours, that simplicity starts to play tricks on your mind. You begin to wonder if you've already passed that same red barn before, or if Iowa just keeps recycling scenery, daring you to notice.

Once we arrived to Aunt Sues, I can tell you this; never in my life have I been welcomed like I was that night. We arrived late, weary from miles of interstate, expecting a sandwich or leftovers.

Instead, Sue and her husband Darrell grilled steaks so good I still talk about them years later. Steaks fit for royalty. The following days were a blur of stories about Dennis: his quirks, his wanderings, and his idiosyncrasies. I do think many people would have considered him a loner, stubborn, eccentric, unconventional, and a maverick. I imagine him showing up at a dinner party wearing a fur coat with some polyester pants, but above all, he is undeniably unforgettable.

My second (paternal meeting) sibling meeting came the next day, when Sue and Darrell drove us out to a park where my brother Rocky was waiting. My heart pounded as I spotted him, this stranger who somehow wasn't a stranger at all. He stood with the same posture as my son.

The anticipation was unlike anything I'd ever felt. It was not like meeting Terri's children, where at least I'd chased a history I already knew. With Rocky, neither of us had even known the other existed until recently. Talk about whiplash! It felt like everything had been dropped on our laps out of nowhere, leaving our heads spinning with questions: What's going on? What did our father do? Who did he do it with? Despite the strangeness and occasional awkwardness, meeting Rocky felt unexpectedly good. My heart was touched. I have a new brother! Tears streamed down my face—tears of joy, but also of disbelief. How could someone so close to me have been hidden all this time?

Rocky was kind, warm, and thoughtful. Rocky could build a castle, travel the world, and still be back in time to pull a perfect oven-baked pizza out of his backyard oven. He loves his family and cherishes them with his whole heart—and it shows in everything he does. He's also a mountain biker, born with that unmistakable gene called "the thrill seeker," which might explain why he treats steep trails the way most of us treat sidewalks.

And then there was Gigi, his wife, nothing short of a marvel. Intelligent, grounded, effortlessly warm, she has a way of making the world feel softer, kinder, and better. She tends her garden, keeps honeybees, and has a chicken coop so charming it could be a dollhouse, supplying fresh eggs every morning that taste like sunshine. And then there's her photography, oh, her photography. I could live inside her images, vicariously wandering the streets and skies she captures on their travels, seeing the world through her eyes, feeling the pulse of each moment she frames.

Now, Etta, their daughter, is remarkable in her own right. Quiet, thoughtful, with a spark that lights up her creativity, she makes her own hand-thrown pottery, each piece a small testament to the wheels turning in that beautiful little head.

She's not loud or brash; instead, you can sense the gears always moving, imagining, inventing and noticing the world in ways that make you smile just watching her. Together, they feel like a small universe of intelligence, care, and quiet brilliance—an unexpected gift I hadn't known I was lucky enough to meet.

For a family outing, Rocky rented a pontoon boat and took us all out on Lake Minnetonka, near where Dennis had lived. Sunlight danced across the water, Etta and Danielle (my new nieces) enjoyed some cousin time together, we laughed. Then, as if on cue, the sky erupted into one of the most breathtaking sunsets I'd ever seen, streaks of orange and violet stretching endlessly, as if heaven itself had decided to show off.

It felt surreal; all of us bobbing on that lake, piecing together fragments of a man we each only partly knew. The joy of discovery pressed against the weight of questions that hovered like shadows. I wondered what did Dad really leave behind? Who was he, to each of us?

The truth is, as much as I longed to imagine how my life might've been different if I'd grown up knowing Dennis, the reality was sobering. He had struggled to be a father to the children he did have. Loving deeply doesn't always come naturally, and neither money nor success can mend the void left by absence.

Yet by the end of that trip, I carried both the ache of what never was and the sweetness of what had been found. I had been given a whole new family: siblings, aunts, cousins, nieces, and even a nephew, all now woven into my story.

Among them are Cameron and Devlin, the youngest of my siblings. (My Rachael calls them her "baby uncles," since they're just a little younger than she. Dave and I met up with them and their mom, Debbie, while traveling through Minnesota, and we spent a lovely afternoon together.

Debbie is an incredibly devoted mother. Both of my younger brothers were born with serious health challenges that required constant care, countless hospital stays, and multiple surgeries, things most people could never endure. But she did. She stood by them through every hardship, every sleepless night. And the boys absolutely adore her, you can see it in their eyes whenever they look at her. The bond they share is one most parents never get to experience.

They shared stories about their lives and about our dad. It seems that in his later years, something in him had softened—whether from failing health or simply the grace of age, I don't know. But he had tried to be a good father to them.

One of my favorite pictures is of Devlin lying asleep on Dennis's chest.

As a mom and a nana, I know how sacred those moments are, feeling the weight of a little one nestled close, resting in the rhythm of your heartbeat, safe in your arms. It's a fierce, tender magic, so deep and consuming it makes you ache with a love that has no end.

Cameron and Devlin are kind-hearted, respectful, and remarkably brilliant, the kind of smart that doesn't boast, but shines steadily, like a quiet flame lighting everyone around it. Their love for their mom and their enduring affection for Dennis runs deep, even though they were so young when he passed away.

One of the greatest gifts they gave me was a short video clip of Dennis. What a wonder it was to see him in motion—to notice the tilt of his posture, the ease in his manner, to hear the timbre of his voice. In that fleeting glimpse, I saw not only the man, but the way he moved through the world, the way others leaned toward him, the life alive in his gestures. Watching it felt like opening a small door in time and finding him still there, if only for a moment.

It was around May 2023. I was going through a rough time, no sugarcoating it. Our house had burned, and we'd been displaced for over a year and a half. I was hobbling around after foot surgery, the result of a slab of granite being dropped on my foot. So, no...I wasn't exactly in the mindset to meet my last unknown sibling.

But then Andrea messaged me.

She was coming to the Antiques Roadshow, just ten minutes from where we were temporarily living. And I mean... antiques? Say no more. I was hooked. Plus, she was fascinating, a real cowgirl sister who trains horses and loves old things. A woman with grit and grace. I had to meet her. Heritage... all the things that tug at the threads of who I am. She intrigued me instantly: a cowgirl with dust on her boots and stories in her pockets. How could I not be curious?

We didn't get to spend nearly enough time together, but the little time we shared, I treasure.

Chapter 19

I Walk on a Path of Color and Light

When I first met my newfound family, they handed me some childhood drawings Dennis had made. I don't know how much interest he carried in art, but the thought of just knowing that somewhere in him was that same impulse, to put pencil to paper, to leave a mark, felt like a tiny thread tying us together. Genes, after all, have their sneaky way of showing up in the oddest of places.

When I visited my sister Camille, her daughter Danielle and I struck up what I can only describe as an "artist-girlfriend-unbreakable-bond." We sat together with Prismacolors, drawing side by side for hours. You shade, you blend, you sharpen the pencil until it's a stub, then you do it all over again. The medium tests your patience like nothing else, but it also rewards you with layers of richness. Suddenly hours have disappeared, leaving nothing but sore fingers, a rainbow of colors, and the faint suspicion that your spine may never be the same again. (If you've ever worked with PrismaColors, you know, each square inch feels like it requires the patience of a monk and the stamina of an Olympic athlete. You don't draw; you endure.)

But somewhere in that endurance, something happens. Beauty slips in. A spark arrives. It's always been that way for humanity. From the chiseled pillars of ancient palaces to Renaissance canvases that glow like windows to heaven, we have always needed beauty. Not just for decoration, but as proof that life can hold wonder. Art is not just about what we see, it's about what we feel when we see it.

Danielle and I laughed, shared stories, and fell into that rhythm only artists understand—that sweet trance where time bends and suddenly you look up and realize the sun has shifted across the whole sky.

Later, Danielle came to stay with me for something bigger, her first really big commission since graduating college. She was nervous, unsure of where to start. We sat in my studio, surrounded by paint swatches and brushes in old mason jars, planning her approach. Oil paints or acrylics? Which colors would sing? Which brushes would glide instead of drag? But art isn't just about brushes and colors, it's about the business too. I taught her the less glamorous side: contracts, legal protections, pricing formulas. How to quantify hours and heart without apologizing. We talked about professionalism and how to carry yourself so clients treat you as an equal, not as a "hobbyist." I saw her notebook filling up with scribbled notes, her shoulders straightening as if she were stepping into her skin for the first time. And when she finished that painting, her client loved it so much that they immediately commissioned another. Watching Danielle glow with confidence, was one of those quiet joys I'll never forget.

I think back often to my own becoming. It took years—long, hesitant years before I ever dared to put my paintings before strangers. My primary focus was being a mom. That was my great commission, the masterpiece that demanded everything from me. Art took second, third, and sometimes last place, because my children and family were my first priority. Some people dismissed me as "just a housewife." JUST? Wow. That's shallow. Whatever. I have always been, and will always be, more than that. Motherhood wasn't a limitation, it was the fire that forged me. Every lunchbox packed, every scraped knee, every late-night prayer for a child's fever, it was all part of the same passion that now spills onto my canvases.

As the children grew, that quiet vow inside me deepened. Commercial art or drafting may be a practical path, but the work felt hollow. It asked nothing of my soul. I wanted awe, wonder, the kind of beauty that makes your chest ache. And so, slowly, I circled back to fine art. It took courage to walk into that first gallery and say, "This is what I have to offer." My heart was pounding, convinced they'd laugh or, worse, politely decline. But to my astonishment, they said yes. My work went up on the walls. My paintings began to sell.

Now, don't picture me as some overnight sensation, far from it. The work has been slow, uncertain, sometimes painfully so. There have been dry spells stretched on like bad weather; rejections, doubts thick enough to choke me. I was no "big time" artist with agents and endless commissions. I was, and am, an artist who sometimes waits weeks for the next call, pinching pennies to do some advertising, and wondering if the world even notices. And yet, little by little, the work has come in. A portrait commission here, a gallery show there. A prominent law firm once asked me for a portrait, and I nearly fell over from the shock. Those moments didn't make me rich, but they gave me something better; proof that the work mattered.

I eventually attended an art school for some courses and took some workshops, learning from some of today's great masters. Somewhere along the way, my process began to evolve. I found myself reaching for materials that shimmered, gold leaf, silver, textures that caught not just the light but something inside the soul. My paintings became more expressive, more intimate. No longer just likenesses, but vessels of emotion. And I realized, I wasn't copying anyone's style. I was reaching toward the same spirit the old masters carried, that hunger for something extraordinary.

Like them, I push myself beyond comfort. I paint through the ache, through the quiet nights, through doubts that whisper I should give up. Something inside me keeps saying: don't stop. I chase a vision not fully seen but deeply felt, like a hum beneath the surface of the world.

Maybe you've felt it too, that longing for something rare, something made with heart and intention. A piece of art that feels like it was meant just for you. That whispers, "you are known, you are cherished." For me, that's the highest calling of art, not just to decorate, but to connect.

In those long hours in my studio, while the paint dries at a pace rivaled only by glaciers (seriously, watching oil paint dry should be an Olympic endurance sport), my mind often drifts. I think of my momma Terri, painting portraits in Jackson Square, hustling for dollars with nothing but raw talent and grit. I think of Dennis, sketching in school when he probably should have been doing math. Their creativity, their stubbornness—they're both a part of me.

That's what I hope my work offers, not just pretty pictures, but keepsakes of emotion and memory. A conversation between you and beauty itself. Something that says: THIS MATTERS.

This journey didn't begin with a brush, it began with wide-eyed wonder, a child tracing light on dusty antiques in her father's gallery. And even now, after all these years, that longing hasn't quieted. It's still here, humming, urging me on.

And so, I paint.

Chapter 20

The Long Road to the Summit

My DNA test results confirmed what suspicion and story had long whispered: Dennis was my biological father. I missed out on knowing him in the way I would have liked, and in truth, my siblings could say the same. He left in his wake a fortune of stories and contradictions, but not the steady warmth of home. He was the flicker of possibility—a lighthouse blinking on the horizon, visible but never nearby.

It remains a mystery how Dennis first crossed paths with Terri. Perhaps it was through Robert Holter, who had also served in the Navy, but no one I spoke with could say for sure. Some stories resist being pieced together—like puzzles with missing fragments that will always remain unfinished.

Dennis Carlson was not a man to be pinned down by titles like "husband" or "father." Those words demanded presence, constancy, the slow grind of patience that domestic life insists upon. And patience, while he had it for business, did not always extend to the people closest to him.

Business, adventure, risk, these were the arenas where he thrived. In the intimate landscapes of family, he faltered. The same man who would risk millions on a shipwreck could not risk tenderness at the dinner table. He could see value in a warehouse of misprinted goods but overlooked the immeasurable worth of simply showing up, of staying, of loving steadily. And yet, how human it is, to shine brilliantly in one sphere and fail in another.

His waters ran deep, and the current could turn fierce without warning. He carried the weight of abandonment, a hunger for control, was it safety he craved or peace? Even with all his success, I sensed he was still searching for a place to belong.

It was Orlyn, his father, who first trained Dennis in the odd alchemy of hustling. They sold combs together, traipsing through barbershops and five'n dime stores. Dennis, still a boy with hair flopping into his eyes, must have carried those boxes with pride. His brothers, Butch and Bruce, sometimes joined too.

They would drive from shop to shop, offering neat little boxes of combs as though they were jewels. The barbershop air was thick with talc and cigarette smoke, the hum of clippers, the spit of men's laughter. Dennis, thin and sharp-eyed, would carry the samples inside like a boy prince delivering tribute.

"Comb, mister? You can't cut hair without one." Sometimes the barbers bought. Sometimes they waved him away. But the ritual mattered more than the sale. His father insisted Dennis hand over the goods, his fingers brushing the barber's, teaching the boy that money wasn't the only exchange in business. There was eye contact, confidence and the weight of trust.

The streets of Minneapolis were merciless in winter, the wind biting through wool coats and settling into the bones. Orlyn would often pull Dennis from school, setting the boy beside him on the road, as though his charm were currency. Together they wandered through barbershops and smoke-filled basements where men gathered to drink, to gamble, to spin their stories into the night. Too many times, Dennis and his brothers curled up in the backseat of a frozen car, their father's laughter drifting from a barroom as the day's earnings dissolved into drink.

Dennis hated it, and he loved it. He hated the smell of mildew in the box, the jail nights with his dad, and the way older men sometimes looked at him, like a stray pup with a sales pitch. But he loved the thrill when a barber cracked a grin and said, "All right, kid, I'll take a dozen."

It was a strange kind of theater, and without knowing it, Dennis was learning his first real performance: the art of the sell. Years later, he named his company C.O.M.B., which stood for "Close Out Merchandise Buyers". People may have assumed the acronym was thought up in a fancy corporate boardroom, but it wasn't. Dennis decided to name it C.O.M.B. in memory of those days spent with his dad.

By 1984, the Minneapolis Star Tribune came calling, dubbing him the boy with the box of combs turned millionaire merchant. C.O.M.B. was now a juggernaut, climbing toward seventy million in annual sales. Not bad for a kid who once peddled combs in barbershops that smelled of Old Spice and disappointment.

But beneath the headlines was the truth: a dropout, scarred by failure and abandonment, hollowed by the grief of losing his father too soon. That wound became his shadow, shaping every gamble and every restless turn of his ambition. From that ache, he carved his place in the world—and out of that place, he built a legend.

By the mid-1980s, C.O.M.B. employed over a thousand people. The stores, with their yellow "Legally Stolen Merchandise" signs, felt part carnival, part bargain-hunter's dream. Was it junk? Maybe. But it was his junk, and he sold it like it was gold.

Dennis himself was a contradiction: wiry, boyish, unpolished, half visionary, half rebel. His hobbies made insurance agents sweat: fast cars, motorcycles, experimental planes. He could've fallen from the sky and laughed about it all the way down.

Behind the showman's grin was a deeper hunger—not just for profit, but for story. Because profit fades, but stories linger. And Dennis was always building one. Beneath the humor was loyalty, memory, and the faint echo of that boy with a box of combs.

Father and son, two versions of the same instinct, diverging like branches from the same trunk. One building an empire of surplus, the other chasing buried legends. Both, in their way, treasure hunters.

Maybe that's why he named it C.O.M.B. Not just as a joke, but as a reminder: empires start small and sometimes ridiculous. They begin with things you can hold in your hand. One day, a boy with a box of combs. The next, a man with a company bearing their name. And in between—a thousand risks, a thousand shrugs, and one hell of a hustler.

Dennis Carlson

Chapter 21

Highways of Hustle, Byways of Dreaming

For me, the irony doubles back: I grew up under the care of Tommy, my adoptive father, who lived with a quest to find treasures, for the Antique Gallery. Two men, unrelated, orbiting my life with obsessions for what lay buried, lost, or hidden. Both chased what shimmered just out of reach, leaving behind what was far more precious.

Was it fate? A cosmic joke? Or perhaps a compass pointing me—the child caught between them—toward the lesson they could not see: that the greatest treasure isn't under the sea or in the market, but in the slow, steady work of being present, of belonging.

And yet, I admire them, for their daring, their mischief, their refusal to accept the ordinary. For showing me, by both presence and absence, what it means to live wildly, and what it costs. Each struggled with life's storms, but like good sailors, they endured. Dennis's story, like Tommy's, is stitched into me. The pirate's compass, the summit, the long view, I stand in both their shadows, gathering the pieces of a map that leads not to gold, but to understanding. Living not in fear, but in search.

Dennis's wardrobe leaned toward shirts left unbuttoned at the neck and jackets that seemed to prefer casual rebellion over boardroom polish. Yet beneath that almost careless exterior ticked the sharp mind of a man who could turn a complaint into a deal, and a deal into a fortune.

Dennis lived in extremes, toggling between boyish wonder and a hardened impatience that warned you not to waste his time. But that was Dennis, half rebel, half visionary, a man who didn't just walk the edge of life but jumped off it. "Dennis never really landed," a friend once joked. "He just kept falling and finding new ways to make it interesting."

Dennis

The MINNEAPOLIS STAR feature (1981) is more reflective, situating him as a hunter of big-game deals, scouring the country for distressed merchandise like a predator tracking wounded prey. Even the photos tell their own story: one of him dwarfed by a telescope, scanning the heavens as if bargains were celestial objects, another of trucks backing into a new store like ships unloading loot.

He also had a way of making failure sound like rehearsal for some greater success.

Sometimes, though, even Dennis couldn't charm his way out of a storm.

A man named Jacobs was behind bringing C.O.M.B. public on the stock market. He was a famed corporate raider—shark, snake, take your pick. Dennis was running with monsters, and the deeper he went, the darker it became. Men like Jacobs didn't build things, they consumed them. They took what shone, stripped it for parts, and left behind the bones.

When Dennis lost control of his company, it wasn't just business, it was personal. It was his identity, his pride, his late nights and early mornings, his sweat in every brick of that dream. He'd believed he'd found his place among giants, only to realize he had been the meal.

The local newspapers called it a deal gone sour, but to him it felt like theft, the kind that didn't just empty your pockets, but hollowed out your confidence. For years afterward, he carried that loss like an invisible limp. He smiled, he joked, he moved on. But deep down, there was a quiet fury—a mix of humiliation and disbelief—that a man could build an empire from nothing and still have it snatched away by a deceitful, untrustworthy peer.

Yet Dennis was not a man who stayed down for long. He had a gambler's heart, and the world was still full of bets to place.

The AUSTIN DAILY HERALD piece (1984) paints him as a hometown business hustler, rolling in truckloads of merchandise, promising bargains that stirred small-town anticipation.

It was the late 1980s when Dennis discovered his next big thrill: the Home Shopping Network. To most, it was a curiosity, late- night television peddling cubic zirconia rings and kitchen gadgets. To Carlson, it was electric. And when it came to business, the man had the patience of a cat stalking a mouse. When the stock market dangled a tasty morsel called Home Shopping Network, Carlson wanted in. The problem was, you couldn't touch a share without going through the velvet ropes of Wall Street. Merrill Lynch, with its polished stockbrokers and the perfect, groomed business look, guarded the door. Carlson, a man who had no time for velvet ropes, wasn't having it.

A man named Michael Prozumenshikov entered the picture. He was a broker with a name straight out of a spy novel and a voice smooth enough to charm squirrels out of trees. Dennis had inquired with him about getting some of the Shopping Network stock. The next day, Michael called back, his tone practically glowing through the receiver. He'd done it—secured ten thousand shares, ready for the taking. Carlson didn't hesitate. "I'll take them all," he said, as casually as if he were ordering a plate of fried chicken instead of claiming a golden key to future millions.

The stock launched, the price soared, and Carlson's gamble spun into a small fortune almost overnight. He poured money into HSN stock, not cautiously but in bold, sweeping buys. The ticker became his heartbeat. He was no longer just watching the network—he was betting his fortune on it. When the HSN stock surged, Dennis's gamble paid off spectacularly. What had once been catalog money now ballooned into something much larger. He was suddenly not just wealthy, but EXTREMELY WEALTHY.

Dennis Carlson's story reads like folklore: the boy-faced millionaire who grumbled at waiters, flies his own planes, and bets the farm on late-night TV. He was equal parts eccentric and genius, a man who built fortunes the way other men build model airplanes—meticulously, obsessively, and continuously with a touch of danger.

Then, as if bored by millions, he sold it all and started sniffing around for the next thrill. Like any boyhood adventure, the very idea of pirates stirred Dennis's blood. Not the cartoonish kind with parrots and eyepatches, but the real ones — hard-eyed men who had once hidden their loot in places no law had touched. To Dennis, pirates were simply the businessmen of another age: ruthless, cunning, and unforgettable. And if their spoils were still out there, it seemed only reasonable that a man like him should help uncover them.

He had a framed clipping about the WHYDAH, Barry Clifford's great triumph of discovery. Barry Clifford (b. 1945) is an American underwater explorer famous for discovering the wreck of the WHYDAH GALLY, a pirate ship that sank in 1717. Dennis was interested in finding the treasures on the sunken vessel. A pirate ship resurrected from the sea floor

— proof that legends sometimes surfaced if you were stubborn enough to look. Dennis didn't talk about Clifford the way other men might have, with envy or awe. No, he grinned about it, as though Clifford was a cousin who had gone ahead and found the best fishing hole. "See," he'd say, tapping the glass, "told you pirates were just businessmen who knew how to hide assets."

So, when word reached him of expeditions, of ships being sought, of wrecks being teased out of salt and sand. Dennis did not hesitate. He listened, he calculated, and then he invested.

It wasn't logical, not in the tidy, accountant's sense of the word. But Dennis had never lived tidily. Logic was for those who wanted guarantees. Dennis wanted adventure wrapped in profit, the thrill of possibly holding in his hands a coin touched by Blackbeard himself.

And it must be said; he had a flair for suspense. He never let on, not fully, just how much of himself he'd tied to those ventures. He would mention them lightly over a glass of bourbon, shrugging as though he'd only wagered on a horse race, but in his eyes, there was always that flicker, that quiet daredevil gleam.

When a competitor accused him of being a vulture, he shrugged. "Better a vulture than a pigeon. At least vultures eat."

Once, while walking through a warehouse, he tripped over a pallet and caught himself on a stack of toilet paper. "You see?" he laughed. "Even when I fall, I land soft."

Business was never only about business with Dennis. He was equal parts strategist and showman, a man who could convince you that the mundane was miraculous.

Suspense seemed to follow him, whether he invited it or not. Deals teetered on the edge of collapse, only to be salvaged at the last minute with a quip or a clever twist. Stories about him circulated in half-whispers, never entirely verified but always delicious. Did Dennis really once buy an entire warehouse of misprinted goods and turn it for profit? That was the trick of Dennis, he blurred the line between truth and possibility so thoroughly that you found yourself enjoying the not-knowing.

One reporter asked why he didn't delegate more. Dennis grinned: "Because I like seeing the faces. You don't forget who you're selling to if you look them in the eye."

For Dennis, the story was never finished. There was always another box to open, another ship to raise, another legend to test.

And, of course, another comb tucked in his pocket — just in case.

Chapter 22

Where the Sky Meets the Road

I don't remember falling asleep that night. I just remember thinking about him, my dad Dennis, the way his story slipped through the cracks of mine, the missing piece I couldn't quite name. I thought about his laughter that I never heard, his eyes that I'd only seen in photographs, and the strange familiarity that tugged at me. Sometimes, missing someone you never met hurts in a way that feels ancient.

People understand the ache of losing a baby you never got to meet. When a miscarriage happens, the world nods in quiet sorrow and says, of course you grieve, of course you miss them. They were meant to be a part of your life, flesh of your flesh. Everyone accepts that love can exist. But when it comes to losing a parent, you never met, the grief becomes more complicated to explain. There are no ultrasounds or baby blankets, just an invisible space where something should've been.

How do you mourn a voice you never heard or the comfort of arms that never held you? The world doesn't always make room for that kind of loss. There are no answers for the questions that never got answered. It's a quieter grief, lonelier, in some ways. It sits deep in your bones and waits to be understood.

For years, I told myself I didn't need to know him. That I was fine without that part of my story filled in. But the truth is, there's always that quiet wondering. Who were you? Did you ever think about me? So, when the DNA results came and he showed up, I didn't really question it. I did try to make some sense of it.

I always wanted my roads to lead to a summit—a place where I could stand at the top and look back over everything I'd traveled through. But then, someone reminded me, "There aren't any mountains in your pilgrimage. Your journey began on the bayous and with the city sounds of New Orleans."

Some meetings never happen in this life, but that doesn't stop the heart from reaching for them. I used to think closure came wrapped in conversation or handwritten letters, but sometimes it arrives in dreams—or maybe something deeper than dreams.

My dreams don't follow logic; they follow longing.

"No mountains. Well, fine. Just forget it!

I guess I'll just have to take a plane ride with my daddy Dennis."

It's funny how, in a dream ~ I just showed up, somewhere between heaven and highway, where the road meets the sky. He was there in the pilot's seat—calm, focused, like flying is the one place he's ever truly belonged.

I appeared in the seat beside him, yeah, it was a little awkward.

"It's a real thrill up here, Dad," I say as the clouds drift by beneath us. "What makes you love flying so much?"

He glances over at me, squinting, like he's trying to remember where he's seen me before. And wondering where I just came from.

"Dad," I'd say softly, "I'm the daughter you and Terri had. The one who grew up in New Orleans."

He looked surprised. I can't blame him. With all the chaos and color of his life, I doubt he expected me to show up unannounced. But honestly, I didn't expect to find him either.

When I look out the window, I see storm clouds forming in the distance, wild, unpredictable, beautiful. Below them, highways twisted and tangled, the very roads that somehow brought me here. I point to them and smile. "Those are the crazy turns I had to take to get to you, Dad. That one over there on the right reminded me of the Zephyr ride at Pontchartrain Beach. That's an ole amusement park we had in New Orleans."

He chuckles and nods. "Yeah... I had a few rough roads myself," he says. "But I'm glad you made it—even if it's just in your dream."

"I am too," I tell him.

There's so much I want to ask. "Where did you meet Terri?" I lean forward, eager. "What drew you to her? What was yall's story?"

He chuckles, in that low, knowing laugh that sounds like it holds a hundred secrets. "Ah, your mama," he says, shaking his head. "That woman could light up a room and quiet a storm at the same time."

I smile, picturing her, fiery, creative self, so full of life and music. He says "She was a free-spirited lady, traveling the country with her children. Living in communes, going on political marches, writing for newspapers, always full of surprises."

Dennis leaned back, his eyes fixed somewhere beyond the window, like he was studying an old ledger he couldn't quite balance. "You know," he said, "relationships aren't all that different from business. You think you've got all the time in the world to make things right, but one day the doors close."

He gave a soft laugh, the kind that carries regret. "I should've managed things better. Spent more time where the returns actually mattered. Instead, I kept waiting for the right moment, thinking I could make it up later."

I stayed quiet, letting him talk.

He rubbed his hands together. "Truth is, I missed a few good opportunities. Family, mostly. I let those accounts sit too long, thinking the balance would hold steady. Figured they'd always be there, you know? But time doesn't hand out dividends for neglect." He looked at me, then a softness creeping into his voice. "If you've got something worth investing in, don't wait for the perfect conditions. Put in the capital while there's still value to grow."

I smiled, feeling the weight in his words. "Sounds like you've learned a few lessons in management."

He nodded slowly. "Yeah," he said, almost a whisper. "Just wish I'd learned them sooner. I should've known - it's more important to be rich in love than to have wealth."

The clouds begin to part, a wash of gold light flooding the sky. I know it's time. "Well, Dad," I say, smiling through the ache in my throat, "I guess this is where I head back." He nods, like he already knows I can't stay long.

"Thank you for meeting me here," I whisper. "For letting me imagine what it would've been like to know you. Maybe this is our way of catching up... between heaven and earth."

The plane levels, and as the wind lifts us higher, I feel something inside me ease, a peace I hadn't known I was waiting for.

"You've still got a lot of living to do," he says.

"Dad," I say quietly, "before I go, there's something I really need to tell you... You have some amazing kids. I've met them all, and they're good, kind, funny, and strong people."

He smiles. "I am so happy to hear that. Maybe I did okay."

I laugh softly, wiping away the tears. "You did more than okay."

"I wish we'd had more time," I whisper.

"Time doesn't end, kid," he says. "It just changes altitude."

He tips his cap, turning his gaze towards the sky. I think I heard him say, "Proud of you, kid," but probably that's just my imagination working overtime.

And just like that, I fade away, back to reality, back to the ground.

"Goodbye, Dad," I say to the open sky. "Thank you for the ride, and for the family I didn't know I was missing."

Chapter 23

At My Journey's End

A Chapter of Emotional Closure

I know the gut-wrenching pain of abandonment, the kind that makes you wonder, why wasn't I loved? Why wasn't I kept? That ache is part of what pushed me to write my story. Life hits hard sometimes—fast and unfair—but it also gives us moments to grab hold of: laughter around a table, a hand that finds yours, the quiet miracle of being seen.

If there's one thing, I hope readers take from my journey, it's this: your life matters. Every heartbeat, every scar, every fragile feeling, it all matters. And maybe, just maybe, by sharing my heart, someone else might find healing in their own story. Proof that broken beginnings don't have to mean broken endings. Good things can come from hardships.

It's definitely been a long and winding road. I've always wanted to understand where I came from. I'm not sure if that longing was because I was adopted or not. I'm not happy that I had to travel through such difficult times to get to where I am now, but I am happy to have found my families.

I am a mixture of all three families, each contributing to who I am—kind of like a hybrid fruit, sweet, complex, and uniquely me.

I am beyond grateful for the love and support that's carried me along this winding road. My life has been given blessings poured out by so many wonderful people.

I am thankful for my husband—

He's my steadfast companion through every season of plenty and the valleys of want, through laughter that carried us and trials that tested us. He has stood beside me with strength, weathering every storm. He has loved me through all the detours, the unexpected turns, and the potholes along the way. Together we have learned that true love is not built upon ease, but upon faithfulness, the daily choosing to walk beside one another, even when the path grows rough.

And to my children, —my heart's own echo—

Ben, Bethany and Rachael, to you I am endlessly grateful.

(You truly are the best kids in the world—just saying.)

I have watched you grow from the wild wonder of childhood into the fullness of who you were meant to be. You've become extraordinary souls, strong, kind, wise in ways that humble me. Each of you welcomes others with love, remains devoted to family, lives with purpose, you're fulfilling your gifts, you are using your talents well.

You each have found a love that complements your spirit, a partner who mirrors the light within you. We love you, Angel, David, and Steven, and are thankful you've joined our family. To see the circle of love widening through all of your lives has been one of the sweetest gifts of all.

The luminous grandeur of love has found its way into our arms, packed into tiny bundles we call our grand-darlings, blessings already here, and more blessings still on their way - gifts from heaven.

One of the dearest, kindest friends I have ever known is Patricia. My book would not be complete without mentioning her.

I believe we are kindred spirits, for both of us were adopted. Yet while I have been blessed to feel the warmth of my birth family, she has never known that connection. My heart aches for her, for the love and belonging she was denied. But it also aches for the family who never knew the wonder of her soul, the brilliance of her heart, the depth of her love.

Pat is a force of light in this world, and even in the absence of what was withheld, she radiates compassion, grace, and warmth that ripple into every life she touches. This world is infinitely brighter because she is in it.

"Thy rod and Thy staff, they comfort me."

That line from Psalm 23 has always lingered in my heart. Years ago, I heard a pastor speak of it in a way I've never forgotten. He said that David, the shepherd boy, may have carved his memories into the wood of his staff—lines and notches marking the stories of his faith. Perhaps one said,

"God helped me slay the bear." Another, "The Lord gave me strength to face the lion."

And when the valley darkened and the nights grew long, David might have wandered back to the hills, the air still and full of the scent of sheep and dust. He could sit with that staff across his knees, run his fingers over the carvings, and whisper prayers into the wind, reminders written in wood, of a God who never failed him. Each mark a monument. Each groove is a testimony.

In many ways, this book is my own rod and staff. Its pages carry the carved record of a life, of the battles survived, the mercies received, the laughter and the tears. When I reread these words, I am reminded of the ways God has met me on every hill and in every hollow. Of the people He has woven into my story: family, friends, the precious souls who've walked with me through shadow and sunlight alike.

There were many other valleys along my journey—times when the storms hit hard. One was a Category 4 hurricane. Another, when our house burned. My husband stood at death's door. We have lost family and friends far too soon.

And then came the collective heartbreak of the COVID years. I don't need to tell you how that was—because I know you know.

Things Seen, Learned, and Experienced on the Journey

Now, from this view above, I can see God's workings woven throughout my story, every detour, every heartbreak, every open door. He was there all along, stitching it together. I've witnessed His hand in ways too real to deny. I've seen prayers answered in the quietest, most unexpected ways. And I know, without a doubt, that God hears us.

So, if you're reading this, I hope it brings you peace. I hope it reminds you that no road is wasted, no story too messy to redeem. God is in it all: every twist, every tear, every heartache, and every triumph.

And maybe, just maybe, when you reach your own summit, or take your own little flight through the clouds, you'll look back and see what I see: grace in every mile.

When you have felt even a touch of His presence, glimpsed a miracle in your life, everything changes. Your foundation becomes sure, and you know that you know, deep in your soul, that God is real.

I have seen and experienced miracles, and I hope with all my heart that you do too.

> **A Prayer**
>
> God, if you are real, show me.
>
> I have a special request - tell Him what it is.
>
> Guide me, hold me, and let me feel Your presence in ways I can understand.
>
> In Jesus name, Amen

When it's the darkest before the dawn, a darker place than

you have ever experienced before,

just know that there is a light at the end of the tunnel,

the light is Jesus.

The Way Through

When you no longer know which way the road bends.

But even there, in the thick of the silence

God walks beside you. You are never truly alone.

The cost of becoming light is learning how to

walk through the dark.

You can't always outrun the storms.

Sometimes you have to stand in it, feel the rain on your face,

and let it wash away what no longer belongs.

I can pass through fire and still not be consumed.

Every trial isn't a punishment. Sometimes it's preparation,

a quiet shaping of the soul.

The Path won't always be clear.

There will be darkness, solitude, and hours.

To love when bitterness would be easier

is to plant seeds of hope in a field still heavy with sorrow,

trusting that someday, light will find them

And one day they'll bloom.

Author: Camille Barnes

Hey there, thank you for reading!

If this story resonated with you, I'd be over the moon if you left a review—it really helps the book find its way to other readers.

Scan the QR code to:

- Share your thoughts
- Take a little trip down memory lane with video clips

Every review, every view, every bit of love you share means more than you know. Thank you for being part of this journey!

https://www.amazon.com/gp/product-review/B0G2T1N5RG

https://www.camillebarnesstudio.com/camilles-story

About the Author

Camille Barnes is a Louisiana-born artist and storyteller who brings the same care and attention to her writing as she does to her hand-painted works of art. With a lifelong passion for uncovering hidden stories—whether in her family, her surroundings, or the everyday moments that often go unnoticed—she weaves memory, reflection, and emotion into every page. Camille's work celebrates resilience, creativity, and the beauty found in both light and shadow, inviting readers to see the world with curiosity, heart, and a touch of wonder.

www.ingramcontent.com/pod-product-compliance
Lightning Source LLC
Chambersburg PA
CBHW011947090526
44580CB00008B/112/J